200
EASY INDIAN DISHES

HAMLYN **ALL COLOUR COOKBOOK**

200
EASY INDIAN
DISHES

SUNIL VIJAYAKAR

An Hachette UK Company
www.hachette.co.uk

First published in Great Britain in 2016 by Hamlyn,
a division of Octopus Publishing Group Ltd
Carmelite House, 50 Victoria Embankment
London EC4Y 0DZ
www.octopusbooks.co.uk

ISBN 978 0 60063 056 2
A CIP catalogue record for this book is available from the
British Library

Printed and bound in China

10 9 8 7 6 5 4 3 2 1

Standard level spoon measurements are used in all recipes.
1 tablespoon = one 15 ml spoon
1 teaspoon = one 5 ml spoon

Both imperial and metric measurements have been given
in all recipes. Use one set of measurements only and not a
mixture of both.

Eggs should be medium unless otherwise stated. The
Department of Health advises that eggs should not be
consumed raw. This book contains dishes made with raw
or lightly cooked eggs. It is prudent for more vulnerable
people such as pregnant and nursing mothers, invalids, the
elderly, babies and young children to avoid uncooked or
lightly cooked dishes made with eggs. Once prepared these
dishes should be kept refrigerated and used promptly.

Ovens should be preheated to the specific temperature
– if using a fan-assisted oven, follow manufacturer's
instructions for adjusting the time and the temperature.

This book includes dishes made with nuts and nut
derivatives. It is advisable for customers with known allergic
reactions to nuts and nut derivatives and those who may be
potentially vulnerable to these allergies, such as pregnant
and nursing mothers, invalids, the elderly, babies and
children, to avoid dishes made with nuts and nut oils. It is
also prudent to check the labels of pre-prepared ingredients
for the possible inclusion of nut derivatives.

contents

introduction

introduction

The subcontinent of India is steeped in history and heritage, with many battles fought and lost, empires built and destroyed, and foreign powers invading and ruling the region. Central to all the dramas that have unfolded are the exotic spices that have been cultivated and grown here for centuries. It is the carefully prepared blends of spices that create the mouth-watering tastes, flavours and aromas of India – considered the spice bowl of the world.

Besides offering a wonderful array of flavours, Indian cooking is extremely healthy. Many herbs and spices used in Indian cooking are well known for their medicinal value. Garlic and ginger, the two most essential ingredients in Indian cuisine, have properties that can help combat heart disease and stomach ulcers. Turmeric is generally one of the best anti-inflammatories known in cooking. The exquisite attributes of the various different spices – such as smoky-rich cardamom, warm mellow cumin, musky coriander, woody-scented ginger, tangy mustard and fiery chilli – all add characteristic flavours and special qualities to countless Indian dishes and curries.

Foreign powers, invaders and rulers from India's history have introduced cooking styles that are still in practice today. The north continues to be dominated by Moghul cuisine, while the east is influenced by tribal, Anglo-Indian, Tibetan and Chinese styles of cooking. In the south, the Syrian Jews influenced the cuisine of Kerala, and in western India, the influence of the Portuguese on Goan cooking and the Persians on Parsi cooking still remains strong. The result is a multi-dimensional, colourful cuisine of richness and depth, with a huge variety of recipes that is virtually unmatched anywhere in the world.

One common misconception is that Indian food is very spicy. On the whole, most Indian dishes are instead a balanced blend of various aromatic spices and herbs. There is nothing more satisfying to me than producing a fragrant Indian meal, and being able to share it with friends and family. I hope that in this book you will find many recipes that suit your palate, and that you soon join the ranks of the millions of Indian food addicts around the world!

fresh aromatics & wet spices

The following selection of fresh herbs and aromatics (coriander, curry leaves, etc.) and 'wet' spices (such as onion, ginger, shallots) is essential when cooking various different curries. Always buy the freshest ingredients you can find.

chillies

Fresh green and red chillies are used in many curries to give heat and flavour. Much of the heat resides in the pith and seeds. If you want the chilli flavour but with less heat, slit the chillies in half and remove the pith and seeds, before slicing or chopping.

coriander

Fresh coriander is used widely in Indian cooking. Often the delicate leaves are used to flavour dishes, but the stalks are also used, especially in curry pastes.

curry leaves

These highly aromatic leaves are used fresh in Indian (especially southern) cooking. They come attached to stalks in sprays and are pulled off the stalks before use. Fresh curry leaves freeze well and can be used straight from the freezer.

garlic

One of the essential flavours used in Indian cooking, garlic is used with ginger and onion as the base for many dishes. It is sliced, crushed or grated.

ginger

An indispensable aromatic, fresh (peeled) root ginger has a peppery flavour and is used in both savoury and sweet preparations.

onions

This humble vegetable forms the base of many curries and dishes. Used sliced or chopped, it is usually slowly fried before adding the other ingredients for a curry. Store onions in the kitchen at room temperature.

shallots

These sweet and pungent members of the onion family are widely used in Indian cooking. The easiest way to peel them is to slice them in half and remove the outer skin.

as an aromatic to flavour rice and curries. You can use the black seeds inside the pods, by crushing them and using in a spice mixture or as a component of a garam masala mix.

cassia

Also known as Chinese cinnamon, cassia has a slightly coarser texture and stronger flavour than cinnamon.

chilli

Whole dried red chillies add the fiery heat to a curry. Dried chilli flakes tend to have a milder flavour and chilli powders made from dried chillies vary in heat – mild, medium and hot.

cinnamon

A sweet and warming aromatic spice that comes from the bark of a tree and is available as sticks or rolled bark. It is also widely used in ground powder form.

cloves

An aromatic dried bud from an evergreen tree. Cloves can be used whole or ground.

coconut milk & coconut cream

Widely used in South Indian cooking, canned coconut milk is easily available, along with coconut cream, and is added to curries to impart a rich, creamy texture. You can make your own coconut milk from the grated flesh of fresh coconuts, by mixing with water, blending and then sieving.

coriander

The pale brown seeds of the coriander plant are available whole or ground, and form the base of many curry pastes and mixes.

store-cupboard dry spices & ingredients

amchoor

This is dried mango powder, used as a souring agent in Indian curries. If unavailable, substitute with lemon juice or tamarind paste.

asafoetida

This plant resin, also known as 'devil's dung', is found in lump or powdered form, and is strong in flavour. Usually used in tiny amounts in lentil preparations, it is believed to counteract flatulence.

cardamom

This spice is usually used whole, in its pod,

crispy fried onions

These can be bought ready-fried and stored in plastic packets or tubs from any good Asian greengrocer or supermarket. If you want to make your own, gently fry thinly sliced onions in a large frying pan with a little oil over a low heat for 15–20 minutes or until golden and caramelized. Drain on kitchen paper until crisp.

cumin

Essential in Asian cooking, these small, brown, elongated seeds are used whole or ground, and have a distinctive warm, pungent aroma. Whole seeds may be dry-roasted and sprinkled over a dish just before serving.

curry powder

Ready-made curry powders are widely available and there are many different varieties (depending on the spice mix). They are usually labelled mild, medium or hot. There are also more specific mixes, such as tandoori spice mix or Madras curry powder.

fennel seeds

These small, pale green seeds have a subtle aniseed flavour and are used as a flavouring in some spice mixtures.

fenugreek seeds

The tiny seeds are usually square and shiny yellow. They are widely used in pickles and ground into spice mixes for curries.

garam masala

Added to an Indian dish at the end of cooking, this mix contains ground cardamom, cloves, cumin, peppercorns, cinnamon and nutmeg.

gram flour

Also known as 'besan', this pale yellow flour, made from dried chickpeas, is widely used for thickening and binding, as well as being the main ingredient in savoury batters.

mustard seeds

Black, brown and yellow, these tiny round seeds are widely used to impart a mellow, nutty flavour. They are usually fried in oil until they pop.

nigella seeds

Also known as black onion seeds or 'kalonji', these tiny, matt black, oval seeds are most frequently used to flavour breads and pickles.

palm sugar

Known as 'jaggery' in India, this sugar is made from the sap of various palms. Sold in cakes or cans, the sugar has a deep caramel flavour and is light brown in colour. It is used in curries to balance the spices.

panch poran

This is a spice blend commonly used in Eastern India and Bangladesh (it means 'five spices') and is made up of cumin, brown mustard, fenugreek, nigella and fennel.

saffron

These deep-orange threads are the dried stamens from a special crocus and are used to impart a musky fragrance and golden colour to rice dishes and desserts.

star anise

A flower-shaped collection of dark brown pods, with a decidedly aniseed flavour.

tamarind paste

Used as a souring agent in curries, the paste from this pod is widely available and can be used straight from the jar. You can also buy it as a semi-dried pulp, which needs to be soaked in water and strained before use.

turmeric

This bright orange-yellow rhizome has a warm, musky flavour and is used in small quantities to flavour lentil and rice dishes and curries. It is widely available dried and ground.

white poppy seeds

Also known as 'khus', these tiny white poppy seeds are used in Indian cooking mainly to thicken sauces and curries.

rice

Rice is the basic accompaniment to many Indian dishes and curries and makes a perfect foil to the spicy sauces. A heat diffuser is an important piece of equipment to use when cooking rice, as it will distribute the heat evenly under the saucepan. The other important item is a heavy-based saucepan (to prevent scorching on the bottom) with a tight-fitting lid that keeps the steam in. If your lid fits loosely, put a clean kitchen cloth between the lid and the pot.

soaking

For most everyday meals, you can get good results without soaking your rice. If using older rice, however, soak it in cold water for 15–30 minutes, which makes the grains less brittle. Soaking is also traditional for basmati rice, as it helps the rice expand to maximum length. Always drain your rice thoroughly.

absorption method

The rice is cooked in a measured amount of water so that by the time it's cooked all the water has been absorbed. As the water level drops, trapped steam finishes the cooking.

The key to this method is figuring out the correct amount of water. As a general rule, use 600 ml (1 pint) water to 275 g (9 oz) basmati or long-grain white rice, but you may need to experiment to find the amount you like best. Brown rices require more water, while shorter-grain rices need less. Keep in mind that more water gives you softer, stickier rice and less water results in firmer rice.

When the rice has absorbed all the water, the top layer will be drier and fluffier than the bottom, which can be very moist and fragile. Letting the rice sit off the heat, undisturbed with the lid on, for 5–30 minutes allows the moisture to redistribute, resulting in a more uniform texture.

cooking perfect rice

1 Rinse the rice in a few changes of cold running water. The rinsing removes loose starch, making the rice less sticky. Drain the rice thoroughly.

2 Calculate how much water you will need (see 'absorption method' opposite) and measure it out carefully.

3 Place your rice in the saucepan with the measured amount of water and bring it to the boil. Cover tightly and reduce the heat to low. After 12–15 minutes, the liquid should be absorbed and the rice just tender. Let the rice sit off the heat, undisturbed with the lid on, for at least 5 minutes.

essential equipment

Cooking Indian dishes and curries does not require any expensive or complicated equipment, but with a few essential items, as listed on the right, you can prepare them in an easy and efficient manner.

saucepans, frying pans & woks

These must have a heavy base to ensure that the food will be heated evenly, without burning or sticking. Make sure the lid fits well. Wide,

heavy-based frying pans are also essential when cooking flatbreads such as rotis.

spice grinders

A pestle and mortar is the traditional method of grinding spices, but an electric spice or coffee grinder works as well. When you have to blend wet and dry spices, a mini food processor or blender is invaluable to give you a smooth, well-mixed mixture with ease.

heat diffuser

This is a disc made from perforated metal, with a removable handle, that sits on top of your heat source and provides an evenly distributed heat.

starters

spiced yogurt soup

Serves **4**

Preparation time **10 minutes**

Cooking time **under 20 minutes**

1 litre (1¾ pints) **water**

500 ml (17 fl oz) **natural yogurt**

3 tablespoons **gram flour**

4 **green chillies**, slit lengthways

1 tablespoon finely grated **fresh root ginger**

1 tablespoon **palm sugar**

1 teaspoon **ground turmeric**

1 teaspoon **salt**

2 tablespoons **vegetable oil**

1 tablespoon **ghee**

2 **dried red chillies**, broken into pieces

8 **fresh curry leaves**

1 teaspoon **cumin seeds**

½ teaspoon **black mustard seeds**

pinch of **asafoetida powder** (optional)

4 tablespoons roughly chopped **coriander leaves**

Mix the measurement water, yogurt and gram flour together in a large saucepan until smooth. Add the green chillies, ginger, palm sugar, turmeric and salt. Bring the mixture to the boil, then immediately reduce the heat to low and cook for 8–10 minutes, stirring often.

Heat the oil and ghee in a small frying pan over a medium heat. Stir-fry the dried red chillies, curry leaves, cumin seeds, mustard seeds and asafoetida powder, if using, for 2–3 minutes or until the seeds splutter and pop.

Serve hot, ladled into warmed shallow bowls, with the spiced oil mixture spooned over and scattered with the coriander.

For Punjabi dumpling & yogurt curry, mix 100 g (3½ oz) gram flour in a bowl with 1 teaspoon each baking powder, salt, cumin seeds, garam masala and black mustard seeds. Add 2–3 tablespoons water, or enough to make a thick, clinging batter or paste. Using wet hands, make small walnut-sized balls of the batter, and deep-fry in batches for 6–8 minutes over a medium heat (about 160°C/325°F) or until puffed up and golden. Drain on kitchen paper. Make the soup as above, stirring in the spiced oil mixture, then add the cooked dumplings. Serve immediately in shallow bowls, scattered with the coriander.

onion bhajis

Serves **4**
Preparation time **10 minutes**
Cooking time **under
 20 minutes**

2 **onions**, halved and thinly
 sliced
200 g (7 oz) **gram flour**
1 teaspoon crushed **coriander
 seeds**
2 teaspoons **cumin seeds**
1 teaspoon **hot chilli powder,**
 plus extra for sprinkling
 (optional)
1 teaspoon **mild curry
 powder**
½ teaspoon **ground turmeric**
juice of ½ **lemon**
150–200 ml (5–7 fl oz) **water**
vegetable oil, for deep-frying
salt
Coriander Chutney (see page
 184), to serve

Place the onions in a wide bowl with the gram flour,
coriander, cumin, chilli powder, curry powder, turmeric
and lemon juice. Season well with salt and gradually add
the measurement water until the onions are thoroughly
coated by a thick spiced batter.

Half-fill a saucepan with vegetable oil and place over
a high heat until the temperature reaches 180–190°C
(350–375°F), or until a cube of bread browns in
30 seconds. Working in batches, spoon heaped
tablespoons of the mixture into the hot oil and cook
for 3–4 minutes, turning once, until lightly browned
and crispy. Drain on kitchen paper.

Sprinkle with a little chilli powder, if liked, and serve
with Coriander Chutney for dipping into.

For spiced potato fritters with chilli tomato
ketchup, replace the onion with 2 potatoes that
have been cut into thin matchsticks. Cook as above
and serve immediately with a chilli tomato ketchup,
made by mixing 6 tablespoons tomato ketchup with
1 teaspoon hot chilli sauce and 1 tablespoon sweet
chilli sauce.

bengali vegetable noodle broth

Serves **4**
Preparation time **25 minutes**
Cooking time **20–25 minutes**

200 g (7 oz) **dried thick egg noodles**
2 tablespoons **vegetable oil**
1 **onion**, finely chopped
1 teaspoon **ground cumin**
½ teaspoon **ground turmeric**
2 **garlic cloves**, crushed
2 teaspoons grated **fresh root ginger**
1 teaspoon **salt**
2 **green chillies**, finely chopped
100 g (3½ oz) **mangetout**, thinly sliced lengthways
2 large **carrots**, cut into matchsticks
1 **red pepper**, cored, deseeded and thinly sliced
2 **tomatoes**, finely chopped
2 tablespoons **dark soy sauce**
1 litre (1¾ pints) **vegetable stock**
1 teaspoon **pepper**
200 g (7 oz) **baby spinach leaves**
6 tablespoons finely chopped **coriander leaves**
1 teaspoon **sesame oil**

Cook the noodles according to the packet instructions, then drain, rinse in cold water and set aside.

Meanwhile, heat the oil in a large saucepan over a medium heat, add the onion and stir-fry for 8–10 minutes or until lightly browned. Add the cumin, turmeric, garlic, ginger, salt and chillies and stir-fry for 1–2 minutes. Add the mangetout, carrots and red pepper and stir-fry for a further 1–2 minutes. Add the tomatoes, soy sauce, stock and pepper, bring to the boil and simmer for 10–12 minutes until the vegetables are tender.

Add the reserved noodles and spinach and bring back to the boil. Stir until the spinach wilts, remove from the heat and stir in the coriander and sesame oil. Serve ladled into wide bowls.

For spicy vegetable noodle stir-fry, heat 2 tablespoons vegetable oil in a large nonstick wok or frying pan and place over a medium heat. Add 1 finely sliced onion and stir-fry for 5–6 minutes. Add 2 teaspoons each finely chopped fresh root ginger and garlic, 1 finely chopped green chilli, 1 tablespoon curry paste and 400 g (13 oz) mixed stir-fry vegetables. Stir-fry for 3–4 minutes, adding a splash of water, if needed, and then stir in 200 g (7 oz) cooked medium egg noodles. Stir-fry for 2–3 minutes until piping hot and serve immediately.

chilli stuffed bhajis

Makes **8**
Preparation time **20 minutes**
Cooking time **about 10 minutes**

8 large **mild green chillies**
vegetable oil, for deep-frying

Bhaji batter
150 g (8 oz) **gram flour**
100 g (4 oz) **rice flour**
½ teaspoon **baking powder**
1 teaspoon **ground cumin**
2 teaspoons **salt**
1 teaspoon **chilli powder**
750 ml (1¼ pints) **water**

Stuffing
2 tablespoons **vegetable oil**
1 teaspoon **fennel seeds**
2 teaspoons **black mustard seeds**
1 teaspoon **cumin seeds**
1 **potato**, boiled and mashed
3 tablespoons finely chopped **coriander leaves**
1 teaspoon **salt**
½ teaspoon **tamarind paste**
1 tablespoon **roasted peanuts**, roughly chopped

Slit the chillies lengthways and remove all the seeds using a small teaspoon. Soak the chillies in boiling water for 5 minutes. Drain on kitchen paper and set aside.

Mix all the ingredients for the bhaji batter in a large mixing bowl with enough of the water to make a thin batter (the consistency of double cream) and set aside.

Heat the oil for the stuffing in a pan. Add the fennel, mustard and cumin seeds and when they pop add the mashed potato, coriander and salt and mix well. Add the tamarind paste and mix well. Sprinkle over the roasted peanuts. Remove from the heat and mash until evenly combined. Using your fingers, stuff the slit chillies with this mixture.

Heat the oil in a saucepan to 180–190°C (350–375°F), or until a cube of bread browns in 30 seconds. Dip the stuffed green chillies in the prepared batter and deep-fry, in 2 batches, for 2–3 minutes or until crisp and golden. Remove with a slotted spoon and drain on kitchen paper. Serve warm with Coriander Chutney (see page 184).

For aubergine bhajis, cut 2 aubergines into 1 cm thick slices. Make the bhaji batter as above and place the sliced aubergines in it. Toss to coat evenly. When ready to cook, deep-fry the aubergine slices as above, in batches, for 2–3 minutes or until crisp and golden. Drain on kitchen paper and serve.

mulligatawny soup

Serves 4
Preparation time **15 minutes**
Cooking time **50 minutes**

50 g (2 oz) **butter**
1 large **onion**, thinly sliced
1 small **carrot**, cut into small
dice
1 large **celery stick**, finely
chopped
25 g (1 oz) **plain flour**
2 teaspoons **curry powder**
900 ml (1½ pints) **vegetable
stock**
1 large **cooking apple**
2 teaspoons **lemon juice**
25 g (1 oz) **cooked basmati
rice**
salt and **pepper**
flat leaf parsley leaves, finely
chopped, to garnish

Melt the butter in a saucepan and gently fry the onion, carrot and celery until soft. Do not allow to brown. Stir in the flour and curry powder. Cook for 2 minutes and pour in the stock.

Bring to the boil, stirring constantly. Reduce the heat, cover and simmer the soup gently for 30 minutes, stirring occasionally.

Peel, core and dice the apple, then add to the soup with the lemon juice and rice. Season to taste and simmer for a further 10 minutes.

Serve hot, garnished with a sprinkling of parsley.

For lamb mulligatawny, cut 500 g (1 lb) boneless shoulder or leg of lamb into bite-sized pieces. Lightly brown the meat for 3–5 minutes in the melted butter before adding the onion, carrot and celery as above. Proceed as above, but increase the cooking time to 45 minutes or longer, until the lamb is tender, before adding the apple, lemon juice and rice.

spiced potato & vegetable snack

Serves **4**

Preparation time **25 minutes**

Cooking time **35–45 minutes**

2 tablespoons **vegetable oil**

200 g (7 oz) **salted butter**

2 **garlic clove**, crushed

2 **green chillies**, finely
chopped

1 large **onion**, finely chopped

2 teaspoons grated **fresh root
ginger**

400 g (13 oz) can **chopped
tomatoes**

200 g (7 oz) **cauliflower**, finely
chopped

100 g (3½ oz) **green
cabbage**, finely chopped

200 g (7 oz) **fresh peas**

1 large **carrot**, coarsely grated

4 **potatoes**, boiled and
mashed

2 tablespoons **pao bhaji
masala** or **medium curry
powder**

2 teaspoons **salt**

1 tablespoon **lemon juice**

4 tablespoons finely chopped
coriander leaves

4 **white bread rolls**, to serve

Heat the oil and butter in a wok over a medium heat. Sauté the garlic and green chillies for 30 seconds, then stir in the onion and ginger. Stir-fry for 8–10 minutes or until the onion is lightly browned.

Add the tomatoes and stir-fry for 6–8 minutes or until thickened. Stir in the cauliflower, cabbage, peas, carrot and potatoes. Add the pao bhaji masala or curry powder. Cover and cook for 15–20 minutes, stirring occasionally. Season with the salt and stir in the lemon juice. Remove from the heat and scatter over the coriander.

Split the rolls in half and lightly toast them. Serve the potato mixture in warmed bowls with the toasted rolls.

For spiced potato & vegetable curry, heat

2 tablespoons vegetable oil in a large saucepan. Add 1 diced onion, 4 crushed garlic cloves and 1 teaspoon grated fresh root ginger and stir-fry for 3–4 minutes over a medium heat. Stir in 1 tablespoon medium curry powder, 3 diced potatoes, 3 diced carrots, a 400 g (13 oz) can chopped tomatoes and 200 ml (7 fl oz) passata. Add 200 ml (7 fl oz) vegetable stock and bring to the boil. Simmer over a medium heat for 15–20 minutes or until the mixture starts to thicken, then add 200 g (7 oz) fresh or frozen peas. Cook over a high heat for 3–4 minutes, remove from the heat, stir in a small handful of chopped coriander and serve immediately with rice or breads.

spiced courgette fritters

Serves **4**
Preparation time **15 minutes**
Cooking time **10 minutes**

100 g (3½ oz) **gram flour**
1 teaspoon **baking powder**
½ teaspoon **ground turmeric**
2 teaspoons **ground coriander**
1 teaspoon **ground cumin**
1 teaspoon **chilli powder**
250 ml (8 fl oz) **soda water**, chilled
sunflower oil, for deep-frying
625 g (1¼ lb) **courgettes**, cut into thick batons

To serve
sea salt flakes
thick natural yogurt, to serve

Sift the gram flour, baking powder, turmeric, coriander, cumin and chilli powder into a large mixing bowl. Season with salt and gradually add the soda water to make a thick batter, being careful not to overmix.

Pour sunflower oil into a wok until one-third full and heat to 180–190°C (350–375°F), or until a cube of bread browns in 30 seconds. Dip the courgette batons in the spiced batter and then deep-fry in batches for 1–2 minutes or until crisp and golden. Remove with a slotted spoon and drain on kitchen paper. Serve the courgettes immediately, scattered with sea salt flakes and thick natural yogurt, to dip.

For spicy raita, to serve as an accompaniment, whisk 200 ml (7 fl oz) natural yogurt until smooth. Add 6 tablespoons finely chopped mint, 1 small green chilli, deseeded and finely chopped, and ½ teaspoon ground cumin. Season with salt, then sprinkle with chilli powder to serve. Other options include adding chopped cucumber, chopped tomato or finely diced red onion to the yogurt mix.

tandoori tofu bites

Serves **4**
Preparation time **15 minutes**,
   plus standing and
   marinating
Cooking time **20–25 minutes**

400 g (13 oz) **firm tofu**,
   drained
vegetable oil, for oiling
sprigs of **flat leaf parsley**,
   to garnish
lemon wedges, to serve

Marinade
100 ml (3½ fl oz) **thick natural**
   yogurt
1 teaspoon grated **fresh root**
   ginger
1 **garlic clove**, crushed
1 tablespoon **tandoori masala**
1 teaspoon **garam masala**
1 teaspoon **ground coriander**
¼ teaspoon **ground turmeric**
2 tablespoons **lemon juice**

Place the tofu between 2 pieces of kitchen paper and set a chopping board or other weight on top. Leave to stand for at least 10 minutes to remove the excess water. Remove the weight and kitchen paper, then cut the tofu into cubes.

Mix all the marinade ingredients in a large non-metallic bowl and stir in the tofu. Cover and leave to marinate for 1 hour.

Put the tofu pieces on a lightly oiled nonstick baking sheet and cook in a preheated oven, 200°C (400°F), Gas Mark 6, for 20–25 minutes, turning halfway through the cooking time.

Serve the tofu cubes, garnished with parsley, with cocktail sticks for skewering and lemon wedges to squeeze over.

For baked teriyaki tofu bites, follow the above recipe to remove the excess water from the tofu, then cut into cubes. For the marinade, mix 2 tablespoons each dark soy sauce and rice wine or dry sherry, 2 teaspoons chopped fresh root ginger, 1 teaspoon chopped garlic and 1 tablespoon each soft light brown sugar and sesame seeds in a large non-metallic bowl. Stir in the tofu, cover and leave to marinate for 30 minutes. Cook the tofu as above, then serve on cocktail sticks, garnished with shredded spring onions.

parsi-style scrambled eggs

Serves **4**
Preparation time **10 minutes**
Cooking time **13–15 minutes**

25 g (1 oz) **butter**
1 **red onion**, finely diced
2 large **garlic cloves**, finely
  chopped
1 teaspoon grated **fresh root
  ginger**
1 **red chilli,** deseeded and
  finely sliced
2 teaspoons **cumin seeds**
1 large **tomato**, deseeded and
  finely chopped
4 tablespoons finely chopped
  coriander leaves
6 **duck eggs**, lightly beaten
4 tablespoons **crème fraîche**
salt
4 slices of **bread**, toasted and
  buttered, to serve

Melt the butter in a large nonstick frying pan over a medium heat, and fry the onion for about 5 minutes until soft but not coloured. Add the garlic, ginger, chilli and cumin seeds and fry for a further 1 minute. Add half the tomato and half the chopped coriander. Stir and cook gently for another 1 minute.

Whisk the eggs with the crème fraîche, and season well with salt. Take the pan off the heat and pour in the egg mixture. Return the pan to a medium-low heat and stir with a wooden spoon until the mixture lightly sets – it should have a creamy texture and will take 6–8 minutes.

Stir in the remaining tomato and coriander quickly to mix well. Serve immediately, while the eggs are still soft and warm, with the buttered toast slices.

For spiced open omelette, melt 25 g (1 oz) butter in a medium saucepan and sauté 1 diced red onion, 1 finely chopped red chilli and 2 diced garlic cloves for 3–4 minutes. Add 6 large lightly beaten eggs to the mixture and scatter over a small handful of finely chopped coriander and 1 finely diced tomato. Cook over a medium-low heat for 6–8 minutes or until the base is just beginning to set, and then place under a medium-hot grill for 2–3 minutes or until lightly golden and just set. Remove from the grill, season and serve cut into wedges.

steamed chicken dumplings

Makes **20**
Preparation time **20 minutes,**
 plus marinating and resting
Cooking time **12–15 minutes**

1 tablespoon **white wine
 vinegar**
1 tablespoon **dark soy sauce**
6 **spring onions,** very finely
 chopped, plus extra to
 garnish
2 **garlic cloves,** crushed
2 teaspoons **salt**
2 **green chillies,** finely
 chopped
200 g (7 oz) **minced chicken**
150 g (5 oz) **plain flour**
5 tablespoons tepid **water**
2 tablespoons **vegetable oil,**
 plus extra for brushing
sweet chilli sauce, to serve

Mix the vinegar, soy sauce, spring onions, garlic,
1 teaspoon of the salt and the chillies in a bowl. Add
the minced chicken and, using your fingers, mix until well
combined. Cover and leave to marinate for 30 minutes.

Meanwhile, sift the flour and remaining salt into a
large bowl. Add the measurement water and the oil and
knead for 8–10 minutes to make a soft dough. Cover
and rest for 15–20 minutes.

Divide the dough into 20 small balls and, on a lightly
floured surface roll each one out into a very thin,
10 cm (4 inch) disc. Divide the chicken mixture and place
in the centre of each disc. Fold each disc in half to make
a semi-circular 'dumpling', tightly sealing the edges by
carefully pinching the folded edges together.

Place the dumplings in a steamer in a single layer,
lightly brush with oil and steam over a high heat for
12–15 minutes or until the chicken is cooked through.
Serve warm garnished with spring onions and with
sweet chilli sauce to dip into.

For Indian spiced steamed pork & prawn dumplings,
place 200 g (7 oz) minced pork and 400 g (13 oz) roughly
chopped raw, peeled tiger prawns in a food processor
with 2 teaspoons each grated garlic and fresh root ginger,
1 teaspoon cumin seeds, 1 finely chopped red chilli and
a small handful of finely chopped coriander. Season well
and process until fairly smooth. Using wet hands, divide
the mixture into 25 portions and form each one into a ball.
Place on a tray, cover and chill for 6–8 hours, or overnight
if time permits. When ready to cook, steam the dumplings
in a large, tiered steamer for 10–12 minutes or until firm
and cooked through. Serve immediately with chilli sauce.

paneer tikka kebabs

Serves **4**
Preparation time **10 minutes**
Cooking time **10–12 minutes**

400 g (13 oz) **paneer cheese,** cut into bite-sized cubes
2 tablespoons **tikka masala paste**
200 ml (7 fl oz) **natural yogurt**
juice of 1 **lime**
2 tablespoons finely chopped **mint**
2 tablespoons finely chopped **coriander**
1 **red pepper,** cored, deseeded and cut into bite-sized pieces
1 **yellow pepper,** cored, deseeded and cut into bite-sized pieces
vegetable oil, for oiling
salt and **pepper**
lime wedges, to serve
Kachumber (see page 186)
warmed chapattis or **naan** breads (optional)

Place the paneer in a wide bowl.

Mix the tikka masala paste, yogurt, lime juice and 1 tablespoon each of the chopped mint and coriander in a bowl. Season well with salt and pepper and pour over the paneer. Toss to mix well and coat evenly.

Thread the paneer on to 8 metal skewers alternately with the pepper pieces. Place on a lightly oiled grill rack under a medium-hot grill for 10–12 minutes, turning them once and basting with any remaining tikka paste mixture, until the paneer and peppers are lightly charred at the edges.

Transfer to a serving platter, sprinkle over the remaining chopped herbs and serve immediately with lime wedges to squeeze over, accompanied by Kachumber and naan breads or warmed chapattis, if liked.

For chicken tikka kebabs, replace the paneer with 4 boneless, skinless chicken breasts that have been cut into bite-sized pieces, and marinate in the yogurt mixture in the refrigerator for 6–8 hours or overnight. Thread on to skewers with the peppers and grill as above. Serve with steamed rice and a crisp green salad.

pea & potato tikkis

Makes **25**

Preparation time **30 minutes, plus chilling**

Cooking time **10–20 minutes**

1 tablespoon **sunflower oil**, plus extra for deep-frying

4 teaspoons **cumin seeds**

1 teaspoon **black mustard seeds**

1 small **onion**, finely chopped

2 teaspoons finely grated **fresh root ginger**

2 **green chillies**, deseeded and chopped

625 g (1¼ lb) **potatoes**, diced and boiled

200 g (7 oz) **fresh peas**

4 tablespoons **lemon juice**

6 tablespoons chopped **coriander leaves**

100 g (3½ oz) **gram flour**

25 g (1 oz) **self-raising flour**

50 g (2 oz) **rice flour**

large pinch of **ground turmeric**

2 teaspoons crushed **coriander seeds**

350 ml (12 fl oz) **water**

salt and **pepper**

Heat the oil in a wok over a medium heat. Add the cumin seeds and mustard seeds and stir-fry for 1–2 minutes. Add the onion, ginger and chillies and cook for 3–4 minutes.

Add the cooked potatoes and peas and stir-fry for 3–4 minutes. Season well and stir in the lemon juice and chopped coriander. Divide the mixture into 25 portions and shape each one into a ball. Chill until ready to use.

Make the batter by mixing the 3 flours in a bowl. Season and add the turmeric and crushed coriander. Gradually whisk in the measurement water to make a smooth, thick batter.

Pour sunflower oil into a wok until one-third full and heat to 180–190°C (350–375°F), or until a cube of bread browns in 30 seconds. Dip the potato balls in the batter and deep-fry in batches for 1–2 minutes or until golden. Drain on kitchen paper and serve warm with Mint Chutney (see below).

For mint chutney, to serve as an accompaniment, blend 100 ml (3½ fl oz) coconut cream, 200 ml (7 fl oz) natural yogurt, 50 g (2 oz) mint leaves, 1 teaspoon caster sugar, 2 tablespoons lime juice and salt and pepper to taste in a blender or food processor until smooth.

tapioca & potato cakes

Makes **15–20**
Preparation time **10 minutes**,
  plus standing
Cooking time **20–30 minutes**

2 **potatoes**, roughly chopped
200 g (7 oz) **tapioca**
250 ml (8 fl oz) cold **water**
2 **red chillies**, finely chopped
1 teaspoon **cumin seeds**
4 tablespoons finely chopped
  coriander leaves, plus extra
  leaves to garnish
vegetable oil, for deep-frying
salt
lemon wedges, to serve

Cook the potatoes in a pan of lightly salted boiling water for 12–15 minutes or until just tender. Drain thoroughly and transfer to a mixing bowl.

Meanwhile, place the tapioca in a bowl, pour over the measurement water and allow to stand for 12–15 minutes, or until the water is absorbed and the tapioca has swollen and softened. Place in a sieve to drain any excess liquid.

Add the chillies, cumin seeds, 1 teaspoon salt and chopped coriander to the potatoes and mash until fairly smooth. Stir in the soaked tapioca and stir to mix well. With wet hands, roll the mixture into 15–20 small walnut-sized balls and then flatten to make 'cakes'.

Heat enough oil for deep-frying in a large saucepan or deep-fryer to 180–190°C (350–375°F), or until a cube of bread browns in 30 seconds. Deep-fry the cakes in batches for 3–4 minutes or until golden brown. Remove with a slotted spoon and drain on kitchen paper. Serve warm, garnished with coriander leaves and with lemon wedges, to squeeze over.

For spicy pea & potato cakes, mix 400 g (13 oz) cooled mashed potato in a mixing bowl with 2 finely chopped red chillies, 2 crushed garlic cloves, 2 teaspoons grated fresh root ginger, 1 tablespoon medium curry powder and 200 g (7 oz) defrosted frozen peas. Season well and mix with your fingers until well combined. Divide the mixture into 20 portions and form each into a cake. Deep-fry as above for 3–4 minutes or until golden, drain on kitchen paper and serve immediately, with lemon wedges to squeeze over.

coriander pork kebabs

Serves **4**
Preparation time **10 minutes,
plus marinating**
Cooking time **10–12 minutes**

**700 g (1 lb 7 oz) pork
tenderloin**, cut into
bite-sized pieces
1 teaspoon **garlic paste**
1 teaspoon **ginger paste**
1 **red chilli,** roughly chopped
4 tablespoons **coconut cream**
2 tablespoons **full-fat natural
yogurt**
1 teaspoon **ground cumin**
½ teaspoon **ground turmeric**
1 tablespoon **ground
coriander**
juice of 1 **lime**
50 g (2 oz) **fresh coriander**
(leaves and stalks), roughly
chopped
1 tablespoon roughly chopped
mint leaves
2 tablespoons **vegetable oil**,
plus extra for oiling
salt and **pepper**
lime wedges, to serve

Place the pork in a wide non-metallic bowl.

Put the garlic and ginger pastes in a food processor
with the chilli, coconut cream, yogurt, cumin, turmeric,
ground coriander, lime juice and chopped fresh herbs.
Pour in the oil, season well and blend until fairly smooth.
Spoon this mixture over the pork and toss to coat
evenly. Cover and set aside until ready to cook.

Thread the pork on to 8 metal skewers, place on a
lightly oiled grill rack and cook under a medium-hot
grill for 10–12 minutes, turning halfway, until cooked
through and tender.

Serve immediately with lime wedges to squeeze over
and crisp green salad leaves, if liked.

For spicy king prawn kebabs, in a large bowl mix
1 teaspoon each crushed garlic, grated fresh root
ginger, ground cumin, hot chilli powder, hot curry
powder, ground turmeric and ground coriander, the
juice of 1 lemon, 8 tablespoons coconut cream and
1 finely chopped red chilli. Add 24 large raw king or
tiger prawns, peeled and deveined but with the tails left
on, season well with salt and toss to coat evenly. When
ready to cook, thread the prawns on to 8 metal skewers
and cook under a medium-hot grill for 5–6 minutes,
turning halfway, or until pink and cooked through. Serve
immediately with a salad and warmed flatbreads.

masala mixed seafood cakes

Serves **4**
Preparation time **10–15 minutes**
Cooking time **12–15 minutes**

200 g (7 oz) **skinless salmon fillets**, roughly chopped
200 g (7 oz) **skinless cod fillets**, roughly chopped
300 g (10 oz) **raw tiger prawns**, peeled and roughly chopped
1 **red chilli**, deseeded and finely chopped
6 tablespoons chopped **coriander**
6 tablespoons chopped **mint**
1 teaspoon **coconut cream**
2 teaspoons **garlic paste**
1 teaspoon **ginger paste**
1 tablespoon **mild** or **medium curry powder**
100 g (3½ oz) **fresh white breadcrumbs**
1 small **egg**, lightly beaten
vegetable oil, for brushing
salt and **pepper**
lime wedges, to serve

Place the chopped seafood in a food processor with the chilli, coriander, mint, coconut cream, garlic paste, ginger paste, curry powder, breadcrumbs and egg. Season well with salt and pepper and blend until well mixed and fairly smooth.

Divide the mixture into 20 portions and, using wet hands (to stop the mixture sticking to your fingers), form each one into a flat 'cake'.

Line a baking sheet with nonstick silicone baking paper and place the cakes on it in a single layer. Lightly brush each with a little vegetable oil and bake in a preheated oven, 220°C (425°F), Gas Mark 6, for 12–15 minutes or until slightly puffed up and lightly golden.

Serve warm or at room temperature, with lime wedges to squeeze over.

For masala seafood wraps, make the mixed seafood cakes as above. Warm 4 large flour tortillas and spread the base of each one with 4 tablespoons South Indian Coconut Chutney (see page 210) or mango chutney. Scatter over a small handful of shredded iceberg lettuce and 2 sliced tomatoes, and top each wrap with 4 seafood cakes. Roll up to enclose the filling, tucking the sides in, and serve immediately.

tandoori prawn & mango kebabs

Serves **4**
Preparation time **10 minutes**
Cooking time **6–8 minutes**

1 teaspoon **garlic paste**
1 teaspoon **ginger paste**
1 tablespoon **tandoori paste**
100 ml (3½ fl oz) **natural yogurt**
1 teaspoon **clear honey**
2 tablespoons **vegetable oil**, plus extra for oiling
juice of 1 **lemon**
24 **raw tiger** or **king prawns**, peeled and deveined (leaving the tails on if preferred)
400 g (13 oz) **mango flesh**, diced
salt
flatbreads, to serve

To garnish
handful of **coriander sprigs**
1 **mild red chilli**, deseeded and very finely chopped (optional)

Mix the garlic, ginger and tandoori pastes, yogurt, honey, vegetable oil and lemon juice in a large bowl. Stir in the prawns and mango cubes, season with salt and toss to mix well.

Thread the prawn and mango pieces alternately on to 8 metal skewers.

Place on a lightly oiled grill rack under a preheated medium-hot grill for 6–8 minutes, turning once, or until the prawns have turned pink and are cooked through. Remove from the grill and serve immediately, garnished with the coriander and red chilli, if liked, along with flatbreads.

For quick tandoori prawn & mango curry, place 1 teaspoon each grated fresh root ginger, garlic, ground turmeric, chilli powder and tandoori paste and 1 tablespoon each ground cumin, ground coriander and palm sugar in a large saucepan or wok. Add 200 ml (7 fl oz) water and 400 ml (14 fl oz) coconut milk and bring to the boil, then reduce the heat and cook, covered, for 8–10 minutes. Add 24 raw, peeled and deveined tiger prawns and bring back to the boil. Add the diced flesh of 2 mangoes and cook for 5–6 minutes or until the prawns turn pink and are cooked through. Season well and serve over steamed basmati rice.

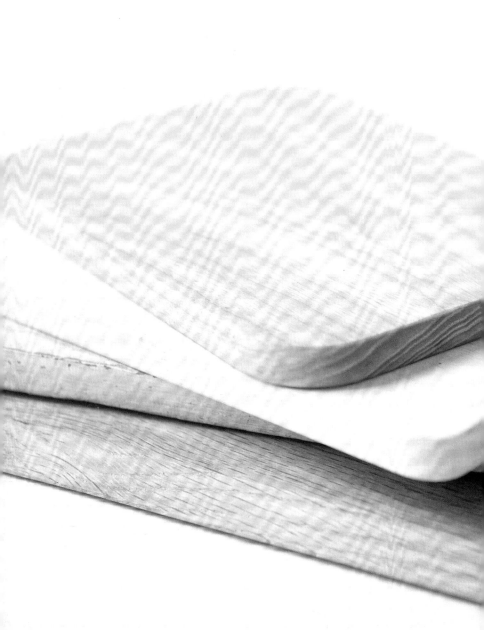

poultry & meat

bombay chicken curry

Serves **4**

Preparation time **10 minutes**

Cooking time **18–20 minutes**

3 tablespoons **vegetable oil**

1 **cinnamon stick**

1 teaspoon **coriander seeds,**
  crushed

2 teaspoons **cumin seeds**

10 **black peppercorns**

3–4 **green cardamoms,**
  bruised

7–8 **cloves**

6 **boneless, skinless chicken
  breasts,** cut into bite-sized
  pieces

Green masala paste

100 g (3½ oz) **fresh
  coriander** (leaves and
  stalks), roughly chopped

25 g (1 oz) **mint leaves,**
  chopped

1 **green chilli**

2 teaspoons **ground cumin**

½ teaspoon **ground turmeric**

1 teaspoon **ginger paste**

2 teaspoons **garlic paste**

400 ml (14 fl oz) **natural
  yogurt**

Make the paste by placing all the ingredients in a food processor and blending until fairly smooth.

Heat the oil in a large nonstick frying pan over a medium heat and add the whole spices. Stir-fry for 30 seconds, then add the green masala paste. Stir-fry for 1–2 minutes and then stir in the chicken. Stir-fry for 1–2 minutes, then turn the heat to medium-low, cover and cook for 15 minutes, stirring occasionally, or until the chicken is cooked through.

Remove from the heat, season and serve with poppadums and Cumin & Pea Rice (see page 196) or basmati rice, if liked.

For green masala lamb kofta kebabs, make the masala paste as above and place in a mixing bowl with 700 g (1 lb 7 oz) minced lamb. Using your fingers, mix until well combined, cover and chill in the refrigerator for 6–8 hours or overnight. When ready to cook, divide the mince mixture into 8 portions, roll each into a long sausage shape and thread on to 8 metal skewers. Grill under a medium-hot grill for 10–12 minutes, turning halfway, until cooked through. Serve immediately with Kachumber (see page 186) and the raita of your choice.

peppered chicken curry

Serves **4**
Preparation time **10 minutes**
Cooking time **20–25 minutes**

4 tablespoons **vegetable oil**

1 teaspoon **black mustard seeds**

8–10 **fresh curry leaves**

2 teaspoons **ground cumin**

1 teaspoon **ground coriander**

1 teaspoon **ground turmeric**

2 teaspoons **salt**

2 tablespoons **pepper**

3 teaspoons **chilli powder**

700 g (1 lb 7 oz) **boneless, skinless chicken thighs** or **breasts**, thinly sliced

400 ml (14 fl oz) **coconut milk**

1 teaspoon **ginger paste**

100 ml (3½ fl oz) water

juice of **1 lime**

chopped **coriander leaves**, to garnish (optional)

steamed basmati rice, to serve

lime halves, to serve

Heat the oil in a nonstick saucepan over a medium heat. Add the mustard seeds and when they start to pop add the curry leaves and stir-fry for 30 seconds. Add the spices, salt, pepper and chilli powder and stir-fry for 1–2 minutes. Add the chicken and stir-fry for 1–2 minutes.

Add in the coconut milk, ginger paste and measurement water, stir to mix well and bring to the boil.

Reduce the heat to medium and cook for 12–15 minutes or until the chicken is cooked through. Remove from the heat, stir in the lime juice and garnish with chopped coriander, if liked, and serve with basmati rice and lime halves to squeeze over.

For spicy pepper beef stir-fry, heat 2 tablespoons oil in a nonstick wok or frying pan and add 1 sliced onion and 10–12 fresh curry leaves. Stir-fry for 3–4 minutes over a medium heat, increase the heat to high and add 700 g (1 lb 7 oz) thinly sliced beef fillet, 2 teaspoons ground cumin, 1 teaspoon each ground coriander and turmeric and 2 tablespoons pepper. Add about 100 ml (3½ fl oz) water and stir-fry for 8–10 minutes or until the chicken is cooked through. Season well, remove from the heat and stir in 1 chopped tomato. Serve immediately with rice or warmed flatbreads.

chicken kofta curry

Serves **4**
Preparation time **15 minutes**
Cooking time **20–25 minutes**

750 g (1½ lb) **minced
  chicken**
2 teaspoons finely grated
  fresh root ginger
2 **garlic cloves**, crushed
2 teaspoons **fennel seeds**,
  crushed
1 teaspoon **ground cinnamon**
1 teaspoon **chilli powder**
cooking oil spray
500 g (1 lb) carton **passata
  with onions and garlic**
1 teaspoon **ground turmeric**
2 tablespoons **medium curry
  powder**
1 teaspoon **agave syrup**
salt and **pepper**

To serve
100 ml (3½ fl oz) **fat-free
  natural yogurt**, whisked
pinch of **chilli powder**
mint leaves

Place the minced chicken in a bowl with the ginger,
garlic, fennel, cinnamon and chilli powder. Season to
taste and mix thoroughly with your hands until well
combined. Form the mixture into walnut-sized balls.

Spray a large nonstick frying pan with cooking oil spray
and place over a medium heat. Add the chicken balls
and stir-fry for 4–5 minutes or until lightly browned.
Transfer to a plate and keep warm.

Pour the passata into the frying pan and add the
turmeric, curry powder and agave syrup. Bring to the
boil, then reduce the heat to a simmer, season to taste
and carefully place the chicken balls in the sauce. Cover
and cook gently for 15–20 minutes, turning the balls
occasionally, until they are cooked through.

Serve immediately, drizzled with the yogurt and
sprinkled with the chilli powder and mint leaves.

For quick chunky chicken Madras, replace the
minced chicken with 750 g (1½ lb) boneless, skinless
chicken breast, cubed, and replace the medium curry
powder with 2 tablespoons Madras curry powder. Cook
as above and add 300 g (10 oz) fresh or frozen peas
for the last 5 minutes of cooking. Serve hot.

goan spiced chicken

Serves **4**
Preparation time **20 minutes**
Cooking time **30–40 minutes**

6 **black peppercorns**
3 **cloves**
2 teaspoons **fennel seeds**
4 **dried red chillies**
1 teaspoon **cardamom seeds**
2 teaspoons **white poppy
  seeds**
2 **cinnamon sticks**
2 teaspoons **salt**
1 teaspoon **ground turmeric**
1 teaspoon **ground cumin**
1 teaspoon **ground coriander**
4 tablespoons **vegetable oil**
1 **onion**, very finely chopped
3 **garlic cloves**, crushed
600 g (1 lb 3½ oz) **boneless,
  skinless chicken thighs**, cut
  into bite-sized pieces
400 ml (14 fl oz) **coconut milk**
300 ml (½ pint) **water**
1 teaspoon **tamarind paste**

To garnish
chopped **coriander leaves**
fresh or **dried coconut
  shavings** or **flakes** (optional)

Place a large nonstick frying pan over a medium heat
and add the peppercorns, cloves, fennel seeds, red
chillies, cardamom seeds, poppy seeds and cinnamon
sticks. Dry-roast for 1–2 minutes, remove from the heat
and allow to cool. Put the cooled spices into a spice or
coffee grinder with the salt, turmeric, ground cumin and
ground coriander. Grind until fairly fine.

Heat the oil in a large saucepan, add the onion and
garlic and cook over a medium heat for 2–3 minutes.
Turn the heat to high, add the chicken and stir-fry for
5–6 minutes or until sealed.

Tip in the spice mixture and stir-fry for 1–2 minutes,
then add the coconut milk and measurement water.
Bring to the boil, reduce the heat to medium-low and
simmer gently for 15–20 minutes.

Stir in the tamarind paste and cook for 2–3 more
minutes or until the chicken is cooked through and
tender. Remove from the heat and serve immediately,
garnished with coriander and coconut, if liked, with
lime pickle and steamed rice, if liked.

For Goan spiced pork & potato, proceed with the
above recipe, replacing the chicken with 500 g (1 lb)
cubed pork tenderloin. When you add the coconut milk
and water, also add 3 potatoes that have been cut into
small bite-sized cubes and continue as above. Serve
with warmed rotis and the raita of your choice.

green masala chicken kebabs

Serves **4**
Preparation time **10 minutes**,
 plus marinating
Cooking time **6–8 minutes**

4 **boneless, skinless chicken
 breasts**, cubed
juice of 1 **lime**
100 ml (3½ fl oz) **fat-free
 natural yogurt**
1 teaspoon finely grated **fresh
 root ginger**
1 **garlic clove**, crushed
1 **green chilli**, deseeded and
 chopped
large handful of finely chopped
 coriander leaves
large handful of finely chopped
 mint leaves
1 tablespoon **medium curry
 powder**
pinch of **salt**
lime wedges, to serve

Place the chicken in a large bowl. Put all the remaining
ingredients except the lime wedges in a food processor
and blend until smooth, adding a little water if necessary.
Pour over the chicken and toss to mix well. Cover and
leave to marinate in the refrigerator overnight.

Preheat the grill until hot. Thread the chicken on to
8 metal skewers, and grill for 6–8 minutes, turning
once or twice, until the chicken is cooked through.
Serve immediately with lime wedges for squeezing.

For red masala chicken kebabs, mix 4 tablespoons
fat-free natural yogurt with 4 tablespoons tomato purée,
1 teaspoon grated fresh root ginger, 4 crushed garlic
cloves, 1 tablespoon chilli powder and 1 teaspoon each
ground cumin and turmeric. Pour over the chicken, then
marinate and cook as above.

chicken & egg wraps

Makes **6**

Preparation time **30 minutes,
plus marinating and resting**

Cooking time **25–30 minutes**

2 **boneless, skinless chicken
breasts,** cubed

2 **garlic cloves,** crushed

1 teaspoon grated **fresh root
ginger**

2 teaspoons **ground cumin**

1 teaspoon **chilli powder**

¼ teaspoon **ground turmeric**

¼ teaspoon **garam masala**

2 teaspoons **tomato purée**

2 tablespoons **natural yogurt**

1 tablespoon **lemon juice**

1 teaspoon s**alt**

1 tablespoon v**egetable oil**

Bread wraps

200 g (7 oz) **plain flour**

1 teaspoon **salt**

1 tablespoon **vegetable oil**

100 ml (3½ fl oz) **milk**

4 **eggs**

To serve

12 tablespoons **Coriander
Chutney** (see page 184)

small handful of **mint leaves**

1 **red onion,** thinly sliced

Place all the ingredients for the chicken in a non-metallic bowl and stir to mix well. Cover and chill in the refrigerator for 6–8 hours, or overnight if time permits.

Make the bread wraps by sifting the flour and salt into a large bowl. Add the oil, milk and 1 egg, beaten, and knead for 8–10 minutes until smooth. Form into a ball, cover and leave to rest for 15–20 minutes.

Meanwhile, thread the marinated chicken on to metal skewers, place under a medium-hot grill and cook for 12–15 minutes, turning once, until cooked through and tender. Remove from the skewers and keep warm.

Beat the remaining eggs lightly. Divide the dough into 6 portions and form each into a ball. Roll each ball into a 16–17 cm (6½–7 inch) disc, 5 mm (¼ inch) thick, on a lightly floured surface.

Heat a nonstick frying pan over a medium heat. Place one disc in the pan and allow to cook for 1 minute. Flip it over and spread 1 tablespoon of the beaten egg all over the surface. Immediately flip it over again, cook for 30–40 seconds and remove from the heat. Repeat with the remaining discs.

Divide the chicken between the bread wraps and drizzle 2 tablespoons of the Coriander Chutney over each one, then scatter over a few mint leaves and red onion. Roll the wraps tightly to encase the filling and serve.

For lamb & egg wraps, replace the chicken with 400 g (13 oz) lamb fillet cut into bite-sized cubes, and proceed as above.

fried chicken parsi style

Serves **4**

Preparation time **15 minutes,**
  plus marinating

Cooking time **15–18 minutes**

1 teaspoon **chilli powder**

1 **green chilli**, finely chopped

2 teaspoons **salt**

1 teaspoon **ground cumin**

1 teaspoon **ground coriander**

2 teaspoons grated **fresh root
  ginger**

3 **garlic cloves**, crushed

1 tablespoon **white wine
  vinegar**

1 teaspoon **palm sugar**

4 tablespoons finely chopped
  coriander leaves

600 g (1 lb 3½ oz) **boneless,
  skinless chicken breasts,**
  cut into bite-sized pieces

vegetable oil, for deep-frying

3 **eggs**, lightly beaten

100 g (3½ oz) **dried white
  breadcrumbs**

Place the chilli powder, green chilli, salt, cumin, coriander, ginger, garlic, vinegar, palm sugar and chopped coriander in a non-metallic bowl. Add the chicken and stir to mix well. Cover and marinate in the refrigerator for 6–8 hours or overnight if time permits.

Heat enough oil for deep-frying in a large saucepan or deep-fryer to 180–190°C (350–375°F), or until a cube of bread browns in 30 seconds.

Put the beaten eggs in a shallow bowl and the breadcrumbs on a large plate. Dip the chicken pieces in the egg, then roll them in the breadcrumbs to coat evenly.

Deep-fry in batches for 5–6 minutes or until crisp, golden and cooked through. Drain on kitchen paper and serve warm with Caramelized Onion Rice (see below), if liked, or raita or chutney to dip into.

For caramelized onion rice, to serve as an accompaniment, heat 4 tablespoons ghee in a heavy-based saucepan and add 3 very finely sliced onions. Sauté over a low heat for 20–25 minutes or until caramelized and lightly golden. Stir in 5 cloves, 4 crushed green cardamom pods, 1 cinnamon stick, 8 black peppercorns and 275 g (9 oz) washed, drained basmati rice. Stir in 500 ml (17 fl oz) boiling vegetable or chicken stock and bring to the boil, then cover, reduce the heat to low and cook for 12 minutes. Take off the heat and allow to stand, covered, for 10–12 minutes before forking through the grains of rice and serving.

tandoori chicken

Serves **4**

Preparation time **10 minutes**,
  plus marinating

Cooking time **20 minutes**

4 large **chicken quarters,
  skinned**

200 ml (7 fl oz) **natural yogurt**

1 teaspoon grated **fresh root
  ginger**

2 **garlic cloves**, crushed

1 teaspoon **garam masala**

2 teaspoons **ground
  coriander**

¼ teaspoon **ground turmeric**

1 tablespoon **tandoori spice
  powder**

4 tablespoons **lemon juice**

1 tablespoon **vegetable oil**

salt

To serve
lime or **lemon wedges**
sea salt flakes

Place the chicken in a non-metallic, shallow, ovenproof dish and make 3 deep slashes in each piece, to allow the flavours to penetrate. Set aside.

Mix the yogurt, ginger, garlic, garam masala, coriander, turmeric, tandoori spice powder, lemon juice and oil in a bowl. Season with salt and spread the mixture over the chicken pieces to cover. Cover and marinate overnight in the refrigerator.

Bake the chicken in a preheated oven, 240°C (475°F), Gas Mark 9, for 20 minutes or until cooked through. Remove from the oven and serve hot with lime or lemon wedges to squeeze over, and sea salt flakes.

For lettuce, cucumber & onion salad, to serve as an accompaniment, combine ½ iceberg lettuce, shredded, ½ mild onion, thinly sliced and separated into pieces, and ½ cucumber, lightly peeled, halved lengthways and sliced. Toss with lemon juice.

potato & minced beef curry

Serves **4**
Preparation time **10 minutes**
Cooking time **20–25 minutes**

1 tablespoon **vegetable oil**
200 g (7 oz) chopped **onion**
700 g (1 lb 7 oz) **minced beef**
2 teaspoons **ginger paste**
2 teaspoons **garlic paste**
2 tablespoons **mild** or
   medium curry paste
500 g (1 lb) **potatoes**, cut into
   1 cm (½ inch) cubes
6 tablespoons **tomato purée**
1 **cinnamon stick**
500 ml (17 fl oz) **chicken,
   beef** or **vegetable stock**
500 g (1 lb) **carton passata
   with onion and garlic**
2 tablespoons **tomato
   ketchup**
200 g (7 oz) r**oasted red
   pepper in brine**, rinsed,
   drained and roughly chopped
small handful of finely chopped
   coriander, to garnish

Heat the oil in a saucepan. Add the onion and minced beef and stir-fry over a high heat for 2–3 minutes. Add the ginger and garlic pastes and the curry paste and cook for a further 1 minute.

Add the potatoes, tomato purée, cinnamon stick, stock, passata and ketchup and mix well. Bring to the boil and cook over a medium-high heat for 12–15 minutes, stirring often. Add the roasted red pepper, bring back to the boil and cook for 3–4 minutes or until tender.

Remove from the heat, check the seasoning and serve garnished with the chopped coriander.

For quick baked minced beef, potato & roasted red pepper pilau, make half the quantity of the above recipe mixture and spoon into the base of a medium-sized casserole dish. Top with 500 g (1 lb) cooked basmati rice in an even layer and sprinkle over a small handful of finely chopped mint. Cover with foil and bake in a preheated oven, 200°C (400°F), Gas Mark 6, for 12–15 minutes or until piping hot.

calcutta beef curry

Serves **4**

Preparation time **20 minutes**, **plus marinating**

Cooking time about **1 hour 20 minutes**

400 g (13 oz) **stewing beef**, cut into bite-sized pieces

5 tablespoons **natural yogurt**

1 tablespoon **medium curry powder**

2 tablespoons **mustard oil**

1 **dried bay leaf**

1 **cinnamon stick**

3 **cloves**

4 **green cardamom pods**, bruised

1 large **onion**, halved and thinly sliced

3 **garlic cloves**, crushed

1 teaspoon finely grated **fresh root ginger**

1 teaspoon **ground turmeric**

1 teaspoon **hot chilli powder**

2 teaspoons **ground cumin**

400 ml (14 fl oz) **beef stock**

salt

Place the meat in a non-metallic bowl. Mix the yogurt and curry powder and pour over the meat. Season with salt, cover and marinate in the refrigerator for 24 hours.

Heat the oil in a large nonstick wok or frying pan and add the bay leaf, cinnamon stick, cloves and cardamom pods. Stir-fry for 1 minute, then add the onion. Stir-fry over a medium heat for 4–5 minutes, then add the garlic, ginger, turmeric, chilli powder and cumin. Add the marinated meat and stir-fry for 10–15 minutes over a low heat.

Pour in the beef stock and bring to the boil. Reduce the heat to low, cover tightly and simmer gently, stirring occasionally, for 1 hour or until the meat is tender. Check the seasoning, remove from the heat and serve immediately, with rice and pickles if liked.

For Calcutta chicken curry, use 4 chicken thighs and 4 chicken drumsticks instead of the beef. Follow the above recipe, replacing the beef stock with chicken stock. Add 100 g (3½ oz) sliced ready-to-eat dried apricots for a hint of sweetness, stirring them in with the stock.

beef & potato madras

Serves **4**

Preparation time **15 minutes, plus marinating**

Cooking time **1¾–2¼ hours**

5 tablespoons **fat-free natural yogurt**

5 tablespoons **Madras curry powder** (see below for homemade)

625 g (1¼ lb) **lean beef fillet**, cubed

2 tablespoons **groundnut oil**

1 large **onion**, thinly sliced

3 **garlic cloves**, crushed

1 teaspoon finely grated **fresh root ginger**

2 **potatoes**, cut into 2.5 cm (1 inch) chunks

400 g (13 oz) can **chopped tomatoes**

400 ml (14 fl oz) **beef stock**

¼ teaspoon **garam masala**

salt

chopped **coriander leaves**, to garnish

Mix the yogurt and curry powder in a large non-metallic bowl. Add the meat, toss well, season with salt, cover and marinate in the refrigerator for 24 hours.

Heat the oil in a large nonstick wok or frying pan with a lid over a medium heat. Add the onion and stir-fry for 4–5 minutes until soft. Add the garlic and ginger and stir-fry for a further 30 seconds.

Reduce the heat to low and add the marinated meat. Stir-fry for 10–15 minutes.

Add the potatoes, tomatoes and stock and bring to the boil. Reduce the heat to very low (using a heat diffuser if possible), cover the pan tightly and simmer gently for 1½–2 hours, stirring occasionally, until the meat is meltingly tender. Check the seasoning and adjust if necessary. Serve garnished with chopped coriander.

For homemade Madras curry powder, to use in the above recipe, dry-roast 8 tablespoons coriander seeds, 6 tablespoons cumin seeds, 1 tablespoon each black mustard seeds and fennel seeds in a nonstick frying pan over a low heat until they begin to pop. Add 8 tablespoons black peppercorns, 4 tablespoons ground cinnamon, 2 tablespoons each ground cardamom, ground turmeric, ground ginger and hot chilli powder, 1 tablespoon cloves and 1 teaspoon grated nutmeg. Continue to heat and stir gently for 2 minutes. Allow to cool, tip the contents of the pan into a spice or coffee grinder and grind to a fine powder. Store in an airtight container for up to 1 month, or in the refrigerator for up to 3 months.

minced beef & pea curry

Serves **4**
Preparation time **20 minutes**
Cooking time **1 hour 20 minutes–2 hours**

2 tablespoons **sunflower oil**
1 large **onion**, finely chopped
3 **garlic cloves**, crushed
1 teaspoon finely grated **fresh root ginger**
3–4 **green chillies**, deseeded and finely sliced
1 tablespoon **cumin seeds**
3 tablespoons **hot curry paste**
750 g (1½ lb) **minced beef**
400 g (13 oz) can **chopped tomatoes**
1 teaspoon **sugar**
4 tablespoons **tomato purée**
4 tablespoons **coconut cream**
250 g (8 oz) **fresh** or **frozen peas**
salt and **pepper**
large handful of chopped **coriander**, to garnish

To serve
lime slices
fresh red chllies

Heat the oil in a large, heavy-based saucepan and add the onion. Cook over a low heat for 15–20 minutes until softened and just turning light golden brown.

Add the garlic, ginger, chillies, cumin seeds and curry paste and stir-fry over a high heat for 1–2 minutes. Add the minced beef and stir-fry for 3–4 minutes.

Stir in the tomatoes, sugar and tomato purée and bring to the boil. Season well, cover and reduce the heat to low. Cook for 1–1½ hours until the mince is tender. Pour in the coconut cream and add the peas 10 minutes before the end of cooking time.

Garnish with the chopped coriander and serve with lime slices and red chillies, as well as rice or naan breads, if liked.

For spaghetti with spicy mince & peas, use this dish as sauce for pasta. Cook 325 g (11 oz) dried spaghetti according to the packet instructions, then drain and divide between 4 plates. Ladle the sauce over and serve.

creamy lamb korma

Serves **4**
Preparation time **20 minutes**
Cooking time **about 45 minutes**

4 tablespoons **sunflower oil**
750 g (1½ lb) **lamb neck fillet**, thinly sliced
1 **onion,** finely chopped
2 **garlic cloves**, finely chopped
2 teaspoons finely grated **fresh root ginger**
65 g (2½ oz) **ground almonds**
1 tablespoon **white poppy seeds**
5 tablespoons **korma curry paste**
150 ml (¼ pint) **vegetable stock**
250 ml (8 fl oz) **single cream**
salt and **pepper**

To garnish
slivered green pistachio nuts
crispy fried shallots

Heat half the oil in a large nonstick frying pan and brown the lamb in batches for 2–3 minutes. Remove with a slotted spoon and set aside.

Pour the remaining oil into the pan. Add the onion, garlic and ginger and cook over a medium heat for 3–4 minutes. Stir in the ground almonds, poppy seeds and curry paste and stir-fry for 1–2 minutes.

Add the reserved lamb to the pan with the stock and cream. Bring to the boil and season well. Reduce the heat and simmer, uncovered and stirring occasionally, for 30 minutes or until the lamb is tender.

Remove from the heat and garnish with slivered pistachio nuts and crispy fried shallots. Serve immediately with rice or warmed breads.

For vegetable korma, sauté 750 g (1½ lb) mixed cauliflower and broccoli florets for 2–3 minutes in 1 tablespoon sunflower oil with 4 finely chopped shallots, 2 finely chopped garlic cloves and 1 teaspoon finely grated fresh root ginger. Stir in 65 g (2½ oz) ground almonds, 1 tablespoon white poppy seeds and 4 tablespoons korma curry paste and mix thoroughly. Add 150 ml (¼ pint) vegetable stock and 250 ml (8 fl oz) single cream. Stir until well combined. Bring to the boil, then reduce the heat to low and simmer gently for 20–25 minutes, stirring often.

kashmiri lamb & fennel stew

Serves **4**
Preparation time **20 minutes**
Cooking time **about 2½ hours**

4 tablespoons **vegetable oil**
2 **onions,** halved and thinly
    sliced
600 g (1 lb 3½ oz) **boneless
    lamb shoulder,** cut into
    bite-sized pieces
4 **garlic cloves,** crushed
2 teaspoons finely grated
    fresh root ginger
1 tablespoon **ground
    coriander**
1 teaspoon **Kashmiri chilli
    powder** or **mild chilli
    powder**
1 teaspoon **salt**
300 g (10 oz) **potatoes,**
    halved
500 ml (17 fl oz) **lamb** or
    chicken stock
200 ml (7 fl oz) **single cream**
4 tablespoons **ground
    almonds**
2 tablespoons crushed **fennel
    seeds**
6 tablespoons finely chopped
    coriander leaves
2 tablespoons finely chopped
    mint leaves

Heat the oil in a nonstick saucepan and cook the onions over a gentle heat for 15–20 minutes, stirring often, until lightly browned. Turn the heat to high, add the lamb and stir-fry for 4–5 minutes until sealed. Reduce the heat to medium and add the garlic, ginger, ground coriander, chilli powder and salt. Stir-fry for 1–2 minutes.

Add the potatoes and stock, cover and simmer over a low heat for about 1½ hours or until the lamb is tender.

Uncover the pan, increase the heat and stir in the cream and almonds. Cook for a further 8–10 minutes until thickened and reduced.

Add the crushed fennel seeds to the saucepan and cook for 3–4 minutes. Remove from the heat, stir in the chopped coriander and mint and serve with Instant Naan Breads, if liked (see below).

For instant naan breads, to serve as an accompaniment, in a bowl, mix 300 g (10 oz) plain flour, 1 teaspoon baking powder, ½ teaspoon bicarbonate of soda and 1 teaspoon salt. Make a well in the middle, add 4 tablespoons milk, 6 tablespoons whisked natural yogurt, 2 tablespoons vegetable oil and about 100 ml (3½ fl oz) water and bring together to make a dough. Knead for 3–4 minutes or until smooth. Divide into 4 portions and roll out into 1 cm (½ inch) thick rounds. Place on 2 large baking sheets, brush the tops with 2 tablespoons melted ghee and bake in a preheated oven, 240°C (475°F), Gas Mark 9, for 4–5 minutes or until lightly spotted and cooked through. Serve warm.

kashmiri lamb chops

Serves **4**

Preparation time **5 minutes**,
   plus marinating

Cooking time **4–6 minutes**

large pinch of **saffron threads**

2 tablespoons boiling **water**

1 teaspoon **ginger paste**

2 teaspoons **garlic paste**

100 ml (3½ fl oz) **natural
   yogurt**

1 teaspoon **ground cumin**

1 teaspoon **Kashmiri chilli
   powder**

1 teaspoon **ground turmeric**

½ teaspoon **ground
   cardamom**

juice of ½ **lemon**

12 **lamb chops** or **cutlets**

salt and **pepper**

sprigs of **coriander,** to garnish

Soak the saffron threads in the measurement boiling water for 3–4 minutes.

Meanwhile, place the ginger and garlic pastes, yogurt, cumin, chilli powder, turmeric, cardamom and lemon juice in a wide non-metallic bowl. Season well and stir in the saffron mixture. Add the lamb to the marinade and toss to coat evenly. Cover and leave to marinate in the refrigerator for 4–6 hours, or overnight if time permits.

Cook the lamb on a smoking hot ridged griddle pan, or under a medium-hot grill, for 2–3 minutes on each side or until cooked to your liking.

Serve with Saffron & Cardamom Pilau (see page 200), or any other rice, and a cooling raita (see below), garnished with coriander sprigs.

For mint & tomato raita, to serve as an accompaniment, whisk 250 ml (8 fl oz) natural yogurt in a bowl until smooth. Stir in a small handful of finely chopped mint leaves, ¼ cucumber, deseeded and finely chopped, ½ red onion, very finely chopped, 1 teaspoon clear honey, ¼ teaspoon toasted cumin seeds and the juice of 1 lime. Season well, cover and chill in the refrigerator until ready to serve.

kholapuri mutton curry

Serves **4**

Preparation time **35 minutes**

Cooking time about **2 hours**

3 tablespoons **vegetable oil**

600 g (1 lb 3½ oz) **boneless mutton** or **lamb shoulder**, diced

1 **onion**, thinly sliced

3 **garlic cloves**, crushed

1 tablespoon finely grated **fresh root ginger**

1 **red chilli**, finely chopped

1 teaspoon ground **turmeric**

12 **fresh curry leaves**

400 g (13 oz) can **chopped tomatoes**

500 ml (17 fl oz) **lamb** or **chicken stock**

100 ml (3½ fl oz) **coconut cream**

3 tablespoons finely chopped **coriander**

Kholapuri curry powder

1 tablespoon **cumin seeds**

2 tablespoons **coriander seeds**

1 teaspoon **ground cardamom seeds**

4 **cloves**

2 **cinnamon sticks**

2 **dried red chillies**

¼ teaspoon **ground nutmeg**

Make the Kholapuri curry powder by placing the cumin, coriander, cardamom, cloves and cinnamon in a nonstick frying pan over a low heat. Dry-fry the spices, shaking the pan, for 1 minute or until fragrant. Remove from the heat, allow to cool and place in a spice or coffee grinder with the chillies and nutmeg. Grind to a powder.

Heat 1 tablespoon of the oil in a heavy-based saucepan over a medium-high heat. Brown the meat in batches for 3–4 minutes. Remove with a slotted spoon and set aside.

Add the remaining oil to the pan and turn the heat to medium. Cook the onion, stirring, for 2–3 minutes until softened. Add the garlic, ginger, chilli, turmeric and curry leaves and cook for 1 minute until fragrant. Add the curry powder, stir well to combine, then return the meat to the pan, stirring to coat in the onion mixture. Add the tomatoes and stock and bring to the boil, then reduce the heat to low and simmer (using a heat diffuser), covered, for 1½ hours or until the meat is tender.

Stir in the coconut cream and most of the coriander, then cook, uncovered, for a further 20 minutes or until the sauce has thickened. Scatter with the remaining coriander, then serve with rice and lime pickle.

For Madras mutton curry, make a Madras curry powder by combining 1 cinnamon stick, 6 cloves, 2 tablespoons coriander seeds, 2 teaspoons each fenugreek seeds and poppy seeds, 1 teaspoon each black mustard seeds, black peppercorns, cumin and fennel seeds, and grinding to a fine powder. Stir in 2 tablespoons hot chilli powder and use in the above recipe in place of the Kholapuri curry powder.

lamb rogan josh

Serves **4**

Preparation time **20 minutes**, **plus marinating**

Cooking time **2 hours**

1 kg (2 lb) **boneless lean lamb**, cubed

400 g (13 oz) can **chopped tomatoes**

300 ml (½ pint) **water**

1 teaspoon **sugar**

2 tablespoons chopped **coriander leaves**, plus extra to garnish

Marinade

1 **onion**, roughly chopped

4 **garlic cloves**, roughly chopped

2 teaspoons grated **fresh root ginger**

1 large **red chilli**, chopped

2 teaspoons **ground coriander**

large pinch of **salt**

1 teaspoon **ground cumin**

1 teaspoon **ground turmeric**

½ teaspoon **ground cinnamon**

½ teaspoon **ground white pepper**

2 tablespoons **red wine vinegar**

Place all the marinade ingredients in a food processor and blend to a smooth paste.

Put the lamb and marinade in a non-metallic bowl and stir to coat evenly. Cover and leave to marinate in the refrigerator overnight.

Place the meat and marinade in a saucepan with the tomatoes, measurement water and sugar. Bring to the boil, then reduce the heat, cover and simmer gently for 1½ hours.

Stir in the coriander and cook, uncovered, for a further 25–30 minutes until the sauce is thick. Garnish with extra coriander and serve with rice.

spiced lamb & mint kebabs

Serves **4**
Preparation time **10 minutes**
Cooking time **10–12 minutes**

500 g (1 lb) **minced lamb**
1 small **onion**, very finely
   chopped
2 tablespoons **garlic paste**
2 teaspoons **ginger paste**
1 teaspoon **chilli paste**
½ teaspoon **ground
   cardamom**
2 teaspoons **cumin seeds**
1 tablespoon **medium curry
   powder**
1 tablespoon **full-fat natural
   yogurt**
100 g (3½ oz) **fresh white
   breadcrumbs**
small handful of finely chopped
   mint
1 small **egg**, lightly beaten
vegetable oil, for oiling
salt and **pepper**

To serve
**Cucumber & Pomegranate
   Raita** (see page 176)
warmed chapattis

Put the minced lamb in a wide bowl and season well
with salt and pepper. Add all the remaining ingredients
(except the oil) and, using your fingers, mix thoroughly
to combine.

Divide the mixture into 12 portions and mould each
portion around a metal skewer into a long sausage shape.

Place the skewers on a lightly oiled grill rack
under a preheated medium-hot grill and cook for
10–12 minutes, turning halfway, until cooked through
and lightly browned.

Serve immediately with Cucumber & Pomegranate
Raita and chapattis (for homemade, see below).

For homemade chapattis, to serve as an
accompaniment, place 400 g (13 oz) chapatti flour
in a mixing bowl with 1 teaspoon salt and ½ teaspoon
sugar. Add 3 tablespoons vegetable oil and work well
into the flour using your fingertips. Gradually add
250 ml (8 fl oz) lukewarm water and mix to form a
dough. Knead for 4–5 minutes, wrap in lightly oiled
clingfilm and leave to rest for 30 minutes. Divide the
dough into 16 portions and form each into a ball.
Flatten each one and roll on a lightly floured surface
to a 15 cm (6 inch) disc. When ready to cook, preheat
a heavy-based frying pan or flat griddle and cook the
chapattis for about 1 minute on each side, pressing
the edges down gently with a clean cloth. Remove
from the heat and keep warm, wrapped in foil, until
all the chapattis are cooked. Serve immediately.

spiced pork patties

Serves **4**
Preparation time **10 minutes**
Cooking time **20 minutes**

500 g (1 lb) **minced pork**
6 **spring onions**, finely
   chopped
1 teaspoon **ginger paste**
1 teaspoon **garlic paste**
small handful of finely chopped
   coriander (leaves and stalks)
2 tablespoons **Madras curry
   paste**
100 g (3½ oz) **fresh white
   breadcrumbs**
vegetable oil, for shallow-
   frying
lime wedges, to serve

Mix the minced pork, spring onions, ginger and garlic pastes, coriander, Madras curry paste and breadcrumbs in a bowl.

Divide the mixture into 12 portions and shape each one into a flat 'cake' or patty.

Shallow-fry the patties, in 2 batches, in a wide, nonstick frying pan for 5 minutes each side, or until browned and cooked through.

Drain on kitchen paper and serve with lime wedges to squeeze over, and a chutney or raita and vegetable of your choice.

For spiced prawn patties, replace the minced pork with 500 g (1 lb) very finely chopped raw peeled tiger prawns, a small handful each of finely chopped dill and coriander (leaves and stalks) and 2 tablespoons each Madras paste and korma paste, and proceed as above.

fish & shellfish

simple seafood curry

Serves **4**

Preparation time **20 minutes**

Cooking time **about 35 minutes**

40 g (1½ oz) **fresh root ginger,** grated

1 teaspoon **ground turmeric**

2 **garlic cloves**, crushed

2 teaspoons **medium curry paste**

150 ml (¼ pint) **natural yogurt**

625 g (1¼ lb) **white fish fillets**, skinned and cut into large pieces

2 tablespoons **vegetable oil**

1 large **onion**, sliced

1 **cinnamon stick**, halved

2 teaspoons **dark muscovado sugar**

2 **bay leaves**

400 g (13 oz) can **chopped tomatoes**

300 ml (½ pint) **fish** or **vegetable stock**

500 g (1 lb) **waxy potatoes**, cut into small chunks

25 g (1 oz) chopped **coriander**

salt and **pepper**

Mix the ginger, turmeric, garlic and curry paste in a bowl. Stir in the yogurt until combined. Add the fish to the bowl, stirring until coated in the spice mixture.

Heat the oil in a large saucepan and gently fry the onion, cinnamon, sugar and bay leaves until the onion is soft. Add the tomatoes, stock and potatoes and bring to the boil. Cook, uncovered, for about 20 minutes until the potatoes are tender and the sauce has thickened.

Tip in the fish and spicy yogurt and reduce the heat to its lowest setting. Cook gently for about 10 minutes or until the fish is cooked through. Check the seasoning, stir in most of the coriander and serve, scattered with the remaining coriander.

For homemade fish stock, melt a knob of butter in a large saucepan and gently fry 2 roughly chopped shallots, 1 small, trimmed, cleaned and roughly chopped leek and 1 roughly chopped celery stick or fennel bulb. Add 1 kg (2 lb) white fish or shellfish bones, heads and trimmings, several sprigs of parsley, ½ lemon and 1 teaspoon black peppercorns. Cover with cold water and bring to a simmer. Cook, uncovered, on the lowest setting for 30 minutes. Strain through a sieve and leave to cool.

spiced prawns with curry leaves

Serves **4**
Preparation time **10 minutes**
Cooking time **6–8 minutes**

700 g (1 lb 7 oz) **raw jumbo
    prawns**, peeled and
    deveined with tails left on
1 teaspoon **Kashmiri chilli
    powder**
1 **green chilli**, finely sliced
3 tablespoons **vegetable oil**
1–2 teaspoons **nigella seeds**
1 teaspoon **cumin seeds**
2 **garlic cloves**, finely chopped
15 **fresh curry leaves**
2 **tomatoes**, finely chopped
salt and **pepper**
basmati rice, to serve

Place the prawns, chilli powder and chilli in a wide mixing bowl, season with salt and pepper and toss to mix well. (The prawns may then be covered and refrigerated until needed.)

Heat the oil in a wok or large nonstick frying pan over a medium-high heat. When hot, add the nigella and cumin seeds. As soon as they begin to pop (a matter of seconds), add the garlic and stir once or twice. Quickly put in the prawns and curry leaves. Stir-fry for 1 minute, then add the tomato. Stir-fry for 2–3 minutes, then turn the heat down to medium-low and let the prawns cook gently for 2–3 minutes, stirring until they just turn pink and opaque and are cooked through.

Serve immediately with basmati rice, poppadums and the vegetable of your choice.

For spiced prawn pasta, cook 350 g (11½ oz) dried penne according to the packet instructions, drain and keep warm. Meanwhile, heat 2 tablespoons vegetable oil in a wok or large nonstick frying pan over a medium-high heat. Add 2 teaspoons nigella seeds and 1 teaspoon cumin seeds. As soon as they begin to pop, add 2 finely chopped garlic cloves and 700 g (1 lb 7 oz) raw, peeled tiger prawns. Stir-fry for 1 minute and then add 2 finely chopped tomatoes. Stir-fry for 2–3 minutes, then turn the heat down to medium-low and let the prawns cook gently for 2–3 minutes, stirring, until they just turn pink and opaque and are cooked through. Stir in the drained pasta with a small handful of chopped coriander, toss to mix well and serve immediately.

kerala prawn curry

Serves **4**

Preparation time **15 minutes**

Cooking time **about 8 minutes**

2 tablespoons **sunflower oil**

3 **garlic cloves**, finely chopped

16 large **raw tiger prawns**, peeled and deveined

1 teaspoon finely grated **fresh root ginger**

1 **red chilli**, finely sliced

150 ml (¼ pint) **water**

100 ml (3½ fl oz) **coconut cream**

6 tablespoons finely chopped **coriander**

salt

lime wedges, to garnish

basmati rice, to serve

Tamarind mixture

1 teaspoon **tamarind paste**

1 teaspoon **hot chilli powder**

2 teaspoons **ground cumin**

1 teaspoon **ground turmeric**

4 tablespoons **water**

Place all the ingredients for the tamarind mixture in a small bowl and stir to mix well.

Heat the oil in a large nonstick wok or frying pan over a medium heat. Add the garlic and prawns and stir-fry for 2–3 minutes.

Stir in the ginger, chilli, measurement water and tamarind mixture. Bring to the boil, reduce the heat and simmer for 2 minutes, then stir in the coconut cream. Gently simmer the mixture for 2–3 minutes, stirring constantly, until the prawns turn pink and are just cooked through.

Remove from the heat, season with salt and stir in the fresh coriander. Garnish with lime wedges and serve immediately with steamed basmati rice.

crispy chilli squid

Serves **4**

Preparation time **10 minutes**,
  plus marinating

Cooking time **10–12 minutes**

500 g (1 lb) **prepared squid
  rings**

vegetable oil, for deep-frying

5 tablespoons **semolina**

5 tablespoons **cornflour**

Marinade

3 **red chillies**, finely chopped,
  plus extra, finely sliced, to
  garnish (optional)

2 teaspoons finely grated
  fresh root ginger

3 **garlic cloves**, crushed

2 tablespoons **white wine
  vinegar**

4 tablespoons **vegetable oil**

1 teaspoon **ground cumin**

1 teaspoon crushed **coriander
  seeds**

1 teaspoon **salt**

Place all the marinade ingredients in a mini food
processor or blender, blend until smooth and transfer
to a wide, non-metallic bowl. Add the squid and toss
to mix well, then cover and marinate in the refrigerator
for 1 hour.

Heat around 8 cm (3¼ inches) of oil in a saucepan
or wok until a small piece of bread dropped in sizzles
immediately.

Mix the semolina and cornflour in another bowl.
Remove the squid from its marinade and dredge it
in the flour mixture. Shake off any excess and deep-fry
the squid in the pan, in 2–3 batches, for 1–2 minutes
or until crisp and golden.

Remove with a slotted spoon, drain on kitchen paper
and serve immediately, garnished with sliced red chilli,
if liked.

For crispy fried scallops, take 25 fresh scallops,
pat dry with kitchen paper and cut them in half (to give
you 50 discs). Place in a large bowl and sprinkle over
1 teaspoon each hot chilli powder, ground cumin,
ground coriander and ground ginger. Season well with
salt and pepper and toss to mix well. Mix 5 tablespoons
each semolina and cornflour on a wide plate. Place
the scallops in the flour mixture and toss to coat well.
Shake off the excess flour and deep-fry the scallops
in 2–3 batches for 1–2 minutes, or until crisp and
golden. Drain on kitchen paper and serve immediately
with a sweet chilli sauce to dip into and lime wedges
to squeeze over.

squid curry with coconut

Serves **4**
Preparation time **10 minutes**
Cooking time **30–35 minutes**

2 teaspoons **salt**
2 teaspoons **ground turmeric**
700 g (1 lb 7 oz) **prepared
   squid rings**
2 tablespoons **vegetable oil**
2 **onions**, finely sliced
4 **green chillies**, slit
   lengthways
3 **garlic cloves,** very thinly
   sliced
12 **fresh curry leaves**
400 ml (14 fl oz) **coconut milk**
4 tablespoons roughly
   chopped **coriander leaves**
basmati rice, to serve

Place half the salt and half the turmeric in a wide bowl
and add the squid. Toss in the mixture and set aside.

Meanwhile, heat the oil in a wide saucepan. Add the
onions, chillies and garlic and stir-fry for a few minutes.
Add the curry leaves and keep cooking for 12–15
minutes over a low heat or until the onion is translucent.

Add the remaining salt and turmeric to the pan. Pour
in the coconut milk, bring to a simmer and cook over a
medium heat for 10 minutes. Add the squid and simmer
very gently for 4–5 minutes or until just cooked through.

Remove from the heat, scatter over the chopped
coriander and serve with steamed basmati rice.

For griddled spiced squid, mix 1 teaspoon salt with
1 teaspoon ground turmeric, gently rub into squid rings
and set aside for 10–12 minutes. Heat a nonstick
ridged griddle pan until smoking. Add the squid rings,
in batches and cook for 1–2 minutes on each side,
then transfer to a serving plate. Meanwhile, finely chop
2 tomatoes, 1 onion, ½ deseeded cucumber, a small
handful of mint and coriander leaves and 2 garlic
cloves and slice 1 red chilli. Place in a bowl, squeeze
over the juice of 2 limes, season well and toss to mix.
Spoon this mixture over the squid, toss to mix well
and serve immediately.

goan clam curry

Serves **4**

Preparation time **6–8 minutes**

Cooking time **about 20 minutes**

3 tablespoons **vegetable oil**

2 **onions**, finely chopped

4 tablespoons **tomato purée**

400 ml (14 fl oz) **coconut milk**

100 ml (3½ fl oz) **water**

2 **green chillies**, slit lengthways

1 kg (2 lbs) **live clams**, washed

1 teaspoon **mustard seeds**

10–12 fresh **curry leaves**

salt and **pepper**

chopped **coriander**, to garnish

Goan spice masala

¼ teaspoon **ground cloves**

1 tablespoon **ground coriander**

1 teaspoon **ground cumin**

2 tablespoons **Kashmir chilli powder** or **mild chilli powder**

¼ teaspoon **ground star anise**

½ teaspoon **ground turmeric**

1 tablespoon **palm sugar**

3 teaspoons **garlic paste**

2 teaspoons **ginger paste**

1½ tablespoons **white wine vinegar**

Mix all the masala ingredients in a non-metallic bowl and set aside.

Heat 2 tablespoons of the oil in a large saucepan over a medium-high heat, then add the onions. Stir-fry for 1–2 minutes and then stir in the masala mix. Cook, stirring, for 2 minutes until aromatic, then stir in the tomato purée and stir-fry for 1 minute.

Stir in the coconut milk and measurement water, add the green chillies and bring to the boil. Turn the heat down to medium and cook for about 10 minutes until the sauce has thickened slightly. Taste for seasoning and adjust if necessary. Add the clams, cover, giving the pan a good shake, and cook over a high heat for 5–6 minutes until they have opened up and are cooked through, shaking the pan occasionally (discard any clams that remain shut).

Meanwhile, heat the remaining oil in a frying pan on a high heat, then add the mustard seeds and curry leaves. Cook for 30 seconds until they begin to pop, then stir into the curry. Garnish with chopped coriander and serve with rice, if liked.

For Goan mussel curry, replace the clams with 1 kg (2 lb) live mussels that have been debearded and scrubbed (discarding any that remain open) and proceed as above.

indian crab salad

Serves **4**
Preparation time **15 minutes**
Cooking time **about**
  5 minutes

2 tablespoons **vegetable oil**
2 **garlic cloves**, finely
  chopped
1 teaspoon grated **fresh root**
  ginger
1 **red chilli**, deseeded and
  finely chopped
6 fresh **curry leaves**
2 teaspoons **cumin seeds**
4 **spring onions**, finely sliced
500 g (1 lb) **cooked white**
  crab meat
½ **cucumber**, deseeded and
  finely chopped
2 **plum tomatoes**, finely
  chopped
juice of **1 lime**
small handful of chopped
  coriander leaves
small handful of chopped **mint**
  leaves
50 g (2 oz) **wild rocket leaves**
salt and **pepper**
lime wedges, to serve

Heat the oil in a nonstick frying pan over a high heat.
Add the garlic, ginger, chilli, curry leaves and cumin
seeds and stir-fry for 1–2 minutes. Stir in the spring
onions and crab meat and stir-fry for 2–3 minutes.

Remove from the heat and stir in the cucumber,
tomatoes, lime juice and chopped herbs. Season well
with salt and pepper and toss to mix well.

Divide the rocket leaves between 4 serving plates,
top with the crab mixture and serve with lime wedges
to squeeze over.

For spicy crab noodles, cook 300 g (10 oz) thin egg
noodles according to the packet instructions, drain and
keep warm. Meanwhile, heat 2 tablespoons vegetable
oil in a nonstick frying pan over a high heat. Add
2 teaspoons each grated garlic and fresh root ginger,
1 finely chopped red chilli and 1 teaspoon curry powder
and stir-fry for 1–2 minutes. Stir in 4 finely sliced spring
onions and 400 g (13 oz) cooked white crab meat and
stir-fry for 1–2 minutes. Remove from the heat and stir
in 1 finely chopped tomato, the juice of ½ lime and a
small handful of finely chopped coriander. Add the
drained noodles, season well with salt and pepper,
toss to mix well and serve.

spicy grilled mackerel

Serves **4**
Preparation time **5 minutes**,
  plus marinating
Cooking time **12–16 minutes**

125 ml (4 fl oz) **natural yogurt**
3 teaspoons **garlic paste**
1 teaspoon **ground cumin**
½ teaspoon **ground turmeric**
1 teaspoon **ground coriander**
2 tablespoons **Kashmiri
  chilli powder** or **mild chilli
  powder**
1 teaspoon **salt**
juice of 1 **lime**
8 **fresh mackerel fillets**
vegetable oil, for oiling
small handful of roughly
  chopped **coriander leaves**

To serve
lime wedges
rice

Whisk the yogurt, garlic paste, cumin, turmeric, ground coriander, chilli powder, salt and lime juice in a bowl.

Make 3–4 diagonal slashes on the skin side of each fillet, add to the yogurt mixture and turn them over to coat well. Set aside to marinate for 5 minutes.

Place the mackerel fillets skin side down in a single layer on a lightly oiled grill rack under a preheated medium-high grill. Cook for 6–8 minutes on each side or until lightly browned and cooked through.

Sprinkle with the chopped coriander, check the seasoning and serve with lime wedges to squeeze over and rice.

For spiced mackerel curry, heat 2 tablespoons vegetable oil in a wide saucepan and add 2 crushed garlic cloves, 2 teaspoons grated fresh root ginger, 1 finely chopped onion, 2 teaspoons ground cumin, 1 teaspoon turmeric and 1 tablespoon Kashmiri or mild chilli powder. Stir-fry for 2–3 minutes, then add 400 ml (14 fl oz) coconut milk and 200 ml (7 fl oz) water. Bring to the boil and add 8 fresh mackerel fillets. Reduce the heat to low and cook for 6–8 minutes or until the fish is cooked through. Remove from the heat, squeeze over the juice of 1 lime and serve with rice.

maharashtrian fish curry

Serves **4**

Preparation time **5 minutes**

Cooking time **about 15 minutes**

6 tablespoons **vegetable oil**

4 **halibut steaks**, about 200 g (7 oz) each

2 teaspoons **cornflour**

4 **garlic cloves**, crushed

1 teaspoon **hot chilli powder**

1 teaspoon **paprika**

½ teaspoon **ground turmeric**

2 teaspoons **ground cumin**

1 teaspoon **ground coriander**

2 teaspoons **salt**

1 teaspoon **tamarind paste**

400 ml (14 fl oz) **coconut milk**

400 ml (14 fl oz) **water**

coriander sprigs, to garnish

To serve
lemon wedges
basmati rice

Heat the oil in a nonstick saucepan and add the fish. Fry the steaks for 1–2 minutes on each side.

Mix the cornflour, garlic, spices, salt, tamarind paste and coconut milk and pour into the saucepan with the measurement water. Bring to the boil, cover and cook gently for 10–12 minutes or until the fish is cooked through and the sauce has thickened slightly (the sauce should still be quite runny).

Serve immediately, garnished with coriander sprigs and lemon wedges, with basmati rice.

For South Indian mixed seafood curry, mix 3 crushed garlic cloves, 2 teaspoons cornflour, 1 tablespoon mild curry powder, 1 teaspoon each ground turmeric, ground cumin, and tamarind paste and 400 ml (14 fl oz) coconut milk in a saucepan, and bring to the boil. Cover and cook gently for 8–10 minutes and then add 400 g (13 oz) raw peeled tiger prawns, 300 g (10 oz) prepared squid rings and 500 g (1 lb) live mussels, scrubbed and debearded. Cover and cook over a high heat for 4–5 minutes or until the prawns have turned pink and the mussels have opened (discarding any that remain closed).

kerala mackerel curry

Serves **4**

Preparation time **10 minutes**, **plus soaking**

Cooking time **15–20 minutes**

4 **dried Kashmiri chillies**, soaked in hot water for 30 minutes

1 tablespoon **paprika**

2 tablespoons **mild curry powder**

150 g (5 oz) **fresh coconut**, grated

200 ml (7 fl oz) **reduced-fat coconut milk**

200 ml (7 fl oz) **water**

2 tablespoons **tamarind paste**

2 **green chillies**, halved lengthways

1 tablespoon finely grated **fresh root ginger**

1 small **onion**, finely chopped

750 g (1 ½ lb) **fresh mackerel fillets**

salt

steamed rice, to serve

Place the drained soaked chillies, paprika, curry powder and coconut in a food processor with the coconut milk and blend to a smooth paste.

Transfer the spice paste to a wide saucepan, add the measurement water, stir to mix and bring to a gentle simmer over a medium-low heat. Add the tamarind paste, green chillies, ginger and onion, and season to taste with salt. Stir and simmer for 2–3 minutes.

Add the fish to the pan, stir once, cover and simmer gently for 10–15 minutes until the fish is just cooked. Serve hot with steamed rice.

For grilled spiced mackerel, arrange 8 fresh mackerel fillets on a lightly greased grill rack, skin side up. Make 3–4 diagonal slashes in each fillet. Mix 2 tablespoons medium curry powder, 4 tablespoons lemon juice, 2 teaspoons each crushed garlic and fresh root ginger and 2 tablespoons coconut cream. Season and spread this mixture over the fish. Cook under a medium-hot grill for 8–10 minutes or until cooked through. Serve immediately.

cochin fish curry

Serves **4**

Preparation time **15 minutes**

Cooking time **about 30 minutes**

1 **onion**, chopped

4 **garlic cloves**, crushed

2 **green chillies,** deseeded and chopped

1 tablespoon **ground cumin**

1 teaspoon **ground coriander**

1 teaspoon **ground turmeric**

small handful of finely chopped **coriander leaves**

200 ml (7 fl oz) **water**

1 tablespoon **groundnut oil**

6 **fresh curry leaves**

400 ml (14 fl oz) **reduced-fat coconut milk**

875 g (1¾ lb) **thick cod** or **halibut fillet**, skinned and cubed

salt and **pepper**

Place the onion, garlic, chillies, cumin, ground coriander, turmeric, fresh coriander and measurement water in a food processor and blend to a smooth paste.

Heat the oil in a large frying pan over a high heat. Add the curry leaves and stir-fry for 20–30 seconds. Now add the blended paste and cook, stirring, over a high heat for 3–4 minutes until fragrant. Reduce the heat, pour in the coconut milk and simmer gently, uncovered, for 20 minutes.

Add the fish to the pan in a single layer and bring back to the boil. Reduce the heat and simmer gently for 5–6 minutes until the fish is just cooked through. Season and remove from the heat.

Serve in warm bowls with steamed basmati rice, if liked.

For creamy prawn & courgette curry, replace the fish with 750 g (1½ lb) raw peeled tiger prawns and 2 courgettes, cut into 1 x 4 cm (½ x 1¾ inch) batons. Proceed as above until the prawns turn pink and are cooked through and the courgette is just tender.

bengali fish curry

Serves **4**
Preparation time **15 minutes**
Cooking time **25–30 minutes**

2 teaspoons **coriander seeds**
1 teaspoon **cumin seeds**
4 tablespoons **mustard** or
   vegetable oil
700 g (1 lb 7 oz) **monkfish
   tail fillet**, cut into large
   bite-sized pieces
2 **potatoes**, cut into finger-
   thick batons
1 teaspoon **ground turmeric**
2 teaspoons **salt**
5 **green chillies**, slit
   lengthways
1 tablespoon **panch phoran
   spice mix**
750 ml (1¼ pints) **water**
steamed rice, to serve

Dry-roast the coriander and cumin seeds in a small frying pan for 1–2 minutes. Cool and finely grind with a pestle and mortar or in a spice or coffee grinder.

Heat 2 tablespoons of the oil in a heavy-based saucepan until it just reaches smoking point. Remove, cool and heat up the oil again on medium heat. Add the fish and fry for 1 minute on each side. Remove with a slotted spoon and set aside.

Heat the remaining oil in the saucepan, add the potatoes and stir-fry for 2–3 minutes. Add the turmeric, salt, ground coriander and cumin, green chillies and panch phoran spice mix and stir-fry for 1 minute.

Pour in the measurement water and bring to the boil. Reduce the heat and simmer for 12–15 minutes or until the potatoes are just tender.

Add the fish to the saucepan and simmer for 3–4 minutes or until the fish is just cooked through. Remove from the heat and serve with steamed rice.

For homemade panch phoran spice mix, to use in the above recipe, place 1 tablespoon each cumin seeds, fennel seeds, nigella seeds, fenugreek seeds and mustard seeds in a heavy-based frying pan. Dry-roast them for 3–4 minutes on a low heat until wildly aromatic. Remove from the heat and allow to cool before mixing and lightly crushing them with a pestle and mortar. Store in an airtight container.

south indian coconut fish curry

Serves 4
Preparation time **10 minutes**
Cooking time **15–20 minutes**

2 teaspoons **salt**
2 teaspoons **ground turmeric**
4 **salmon fillets** or **steaks**,
   about 200 g (7 oz) each
2 tablespoons **vegetable oil**
2 **onions**, finely sliced
4 **green chillies**, slit
   lengthways
3 **garlic cloves**, very thinly
   sliced
12 **fresh curry leaves**
400 ml (14 fl oz) **coconut milk**
100 ml (3½ fl oz) **water**
4 tablespoons finely chopped
   coriander leaves
juice of **1 lime**
basmati rice, to serve

Place half the salt and half the turmeric in a wide bowl and add the salmon. Toss in the mixture and set aside.

Heat the oil in a wide nonstick saucepan. Add the onions, chillies, garlic and curry leaves and stir-fry over a medium-low heat for 6–8 minutes or until the onion is translucent.

Add the remaining salt and turmeric to the pan. Pour in the coconut milk and measurement water and bring to the boil. Add the salmon, in a single layer, reduce the heat to medium and simmer for 6–8 minutes, turning the fish halfway, until just cooked through.

Stir in the lime juice and serve, scattered with the coriander, with basmati rice.

For grilled spiced halibut with salsa, mix 1 teaspoon salt with 1 teaspoon ground turmeric and gently rub into 4 halibut fillets, about 200 g (7 oz) each. Lightly brush the fish with vegetable oil and place under a medium-hot grill for 8–10 minutes or until cooked through. Meanwhile, in a bowl, mix ½ finely diced red onion, 2 finely diced tomatoes, 2 crushed garlic cloves and 1 finely diced green chilli. Squeeze over the juice of 2 limes and season well with salt. When ready to serve, place the grilled fish on warmed plates and spoon over the spicy salsa.

monkfish tikka kebabs

Serves **4**

Preparation time **15 minutes, plus marinating**

Cooking time **8–10 minutes**

750 g (1½ lb) **monkfish tail fillet,** cubed

2 **red peppers**, cored, deseeded and cubed

2 **yellow peppers**, cored, deseeded and cubed

salt and p**epper**

chopped **coriander** and **mint leaves**, to garnish

lime wedges, to serve

Tikka marinade

350 ml (12 fl oz) **fat-free natural yogurt**

2 tablespoons finely grated **onion**

1 tablespoon finely grated garlic

1 tablespoon finely grated **fresh root ginger**

juice of 2 **limes**

3 tablespoons **tikka curry powder**

Mix all the marinade ingredients in a large non-metallic bowl. Add the fish and peppers, season well and toss to coat evenly. Cover and marinate in the refrigerator for 1–2 hours.

Preheat a grill or barbecue until hot. Thread the fish and peppers on to 8 metal skewers and grill for 4–5 minutes on each side until the fish is just cooked through.

Serve immediately, garnished with chopped coriander and mint, with lime wedges for squeezing over.

For monkfish tikka wraps, cook the fish and peppers as above and remove from the skewers. Warm 8 medium chapattis or corn tortillas and top each one with a small handful of shredded lettuce. Divide the fish and peppers between them, drizzle each with a little fat-free fromage frais, wrap up and serve.

baked banana-leaf fish

Serves **4**

Preparation time **15 minutes**

Cooking time **12–15 minutes**

4 **thick salmon fillets**, about
200 g (7oz) each, skinned

2 teaspoons **ground turmeric**

fresh banana leaves,
for wrapping (available
from Asian grocers or
supermarkets)

Spice paste

2 teaspoons **ground cumin**

2 teaspoons **ground
coriander**

1½ teaspoons **palm sugar**

100 g (3½ oz) **coconut cream**

100 g (3½ oz) **coconut**,
freshly grated (thawed if
frozen)

4 **red chillies**, deseeded and
chopped

100 g (3½ oz) fresh **coriander**
(stalks and leaves)

25 g (1 oz) **mint leaves**,
chopped

2 teaspoons **garlic paste**

1 teaspoon **ginger paste**

4 tablespoons **vegetable oil**

juice of 2 **limes**

2 teaspoons **salt**

Place the fish fillets in a single layer on a plate and
sprinkle over the turmeric. Rub into the fish and then
set aside.

Make the spice paste by putting all the ingredients in
a food processor and blending until fairly smooth.

Cut the banana leaves into 4 x 25 cm (10 inch)
squares, then dip them into a pan of very hot water for
a few seconds to soften them. Wipe dry with kitchen
paper and arrange on a work surface.

Apply the spice paste liberally to both sides of each
piece of fish. Place a piece of fish on each banana leaf
and wrap up like a parcel, securing the parcels with
bamboo skewers or string. Place on a baking sheet and
bake in a preheated oven, 200°C (400°F), Gas Mark 6,
for 12–15 minutes until cooked through.

Serve hot with Kachumber (see page 186), Red Lentil
Curry & Spiced Oil (see page 140) and rice, if liked.

For green chutney prawn curry, make the spice paste
as above. Heat 2 tablespoons vegetable oil in a large
wok or frying pan and when hot add the spice paste
and stir-fry for 2–3 minutes. Add 500 ml (17 fl oz) fish
or vegetable stock and bring to the boil. Stir in 700 g
(1 lb 7 oz) raw peeled tiger prawns and bring back to
the boil. Reduce the heat to medium and cook for
6–8 minutes or until the prawns turn pink and are
cooked through. Remove from the heat and serve
with basmati rice.

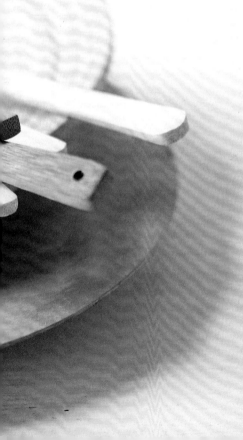

vegetables
& pulses

vegetable curry with poppy seeds

Serves **4**

Preparation time **30 minutes**, **plus soaking**

Cooking time **30–35 minutes**

6 tablespoons **white poppy seeds**

3 tablespoons **mustard seeds**

2 teaspoons grated **fresh root ginger**

4 tablespoons **vegetable oil**

2 **green chillies**, split lengthways

1 tablespoon **panch phoran spice mix**

400 g (13 oz) **butternut squash flesh**, cut into 1.5 cm (¾ inch) cubes

2 **potatoes**, cut into 1.5 cm (¾ inch) cubes

1 **aubergine**, cut into 1.5 cm (¾ inch) cubes

1 **courgette**, cut into 1.5 cm (3/4 inch) cubes

1 **carrot**, cut into 1.5 cm (¾ inch) cubes

1 **tomato**, finely chopped

100 g (3½ oz) **peas**

400 ml (14 fl oz) **water**

¼ teaspoon **ground turmeric**

2 teaspoons **salt**

1 teaspoon **palm sugar**

8 tablespoons **milk**

Soak the white poppy seeds and 2 tablespoons of the black mustard seeds in warm water for 1 hour. Drain and blend with the ginger in a mini food processor or blender to make a paste.

Heat the oil in a large frying pan and add the remaining mustard seeds and the green chillies. When the seeds start to pop, add the panch phoran spice mix and all the vegetables. Add half the measurement water, stir to mix well, cover tightly and cook over a medium heat for 10–12 minutes, stirring often.

Add half the mustard paste, the turmeric, salt and the remainder of the water and cook on a medium-low heat for another 10–15 minutes, stirring often. Add the remainder of the mustard paste, the palm sugar and milk and cook for 5 minutes or until the vegetables are tender. Serve hot with Lemon Rice, if liked (see below).

For lemon rice, to serve as an accompaniment, heat 2 tablespoons vegetable oil in a nonstick saucepan over a medium heat. Add 12 fresh curry leaves, 1 dried red chilli, 1 cinnamon stick, 4 cloves, 4–6 lightly crushed green cardamom pods, 2 teaspoons cumin seeds and 1 teaspoon turmeric. Stir-fry for 20–30 seconds, then add 250 g (8 oz) washed, drained basmati rice. Stir-fry for 2 minutes. Add the juice of 1 lemon and 500 ml (17 fl oz) boiling water, and season well with salt and pepper. Bring to the boil, cover the pan tightly and reduce the heat to low. Cook for 10–12 minutes, then remove from the heat and leave to stand, covered, for 10–15 minutes. To serve, fluff the rice with a fork and check the seasoning. Serve hot, garnished with coriander.

spiced aubergine mash

Serves 4
Preparation time **25 minutes**
Cooking time **45–50 minutes**

4 large **aubergines**
2 tablespoons **vegetable oil**
60 g (2¼ oz) **butter**
2 **onions**, finely chopped
2 teaspoons grated **fresh root
 ginger**
4 **garlic cloves**, crushed
2 **green chillies**, finely sliced
3 **tomatoes**, finely chopped
2 teaspoons **salt**
1 teaspoon **chilli powder**
1 teaspoon **smoked paprika**
2 teaspoons **ground
 coriander**
1 teaspoon **ground cumin**
1 teaspoon **ground turmeric**
½ teaspoon **garam masala**
6 tablespoons finely chopped
 coriander leaves
parathas or **pilau rice**, to
 serve

Roast the aubergines over an open flame on the hob or under a medium-hot grill for 20 minutes, turning, until the skin blackens and chars. To check they are cooked, pierce them with the back of a spoon; if it enters the aubergine like soft butter, it is done. Allow to cool, then remove the skin and roughly mash the pulp. Set aside.

Heat the oil and butter in a large nonstick frying pan and add the chopped onions. Sauté for 5–6 minutes until softened. Add the ginger, garlic and green chillies and stir-fry for 1–2 minutes. Stir in the tomatoes and salt and cook for 12–15 minutes.

Stir in the chilli powder, paprika, ground coriander, cumin and turmeric. Stir in the reserved aubergine flesh and cook for 3–4 minutes. Stir in the garam masala and chopped coriander leaves.

Remove from the heat and serve immediately with parathas or pilau rice.

For spicy grilled aubergines, cut 2 aubergines into 1 cm (½ inch) thick slices and brush with vegetable oil. Heat a nonstick ridged griddle pan until smoking, add the aubergines and cook in batches for 2–3 minutes on each side or until softened. Transfer to a baking sheet and place in a preheated oven, 200°C (400°F), Gas Mark 6, for 6–8 minutes. Meanwhile, finely chop 2 tomatoes and place in a bowl with 8 tablespoons sweet chilli sauce, 1 finely chopped red chilli, a small handful each chopped mint and coriander leaves, 6 finely sliced spring onions and the juice of 2 lemons. Season and stir to mix well. Place the aubergine slices on a serving platter and spoon over the tomato and herb mixture. Serve immediately.

beetroot & coconut curry

Serves **4**
Preparation time **10 minutes**
Cooking time **about
20 minutes**

2 tablespoons **vegetable oil**
¼ teaspoon **black mustard
seeds**
1 **onion**, chopped
2 **garlic cloves**, chopped
2 **green chillies**, deseeded
(if liked) and sliced
2 **bay leaves**
¼ teaspoon **ground turmeric**
2 teaspoons **cumin seeds**
1 **cinnamon stick**
400 g (13 oz) **raw beetroot**,
cut into thin matchsticks
2 **tomatoes,** roughly chopped
200 ml (7 fl oz) **water**
200 ml (7 fl oz) **coconut milk**
juice of 1 **lime**
salt
chopped **coriander leaves**,
to garnish
basmati rice, to serve

Heat the oil in a wide frying pan, then add the mustard seeds. As soon as they begin to pop, add the onion, garlic and chillies and fry for 1–2 minutes until the onion has softened. Add the bay leaves, turmeric, cumin seeds, cinnamon and beetroot and fry for a further 1–2 minutes.

Add the tomatoes, the measurement water and a pinch of salt. Leave to simmer for 12–15 minutes, stirring occasionally, or until the beetroot is tender.

Stir in the coconut milk and let it simmer for another 1–2 minutes until the sauce has thickened. Stir in the lime juice, taste and adjust the seasoning and serve with basmati rice, garnished with the chopped coriander.

For spiced roasted beetroot, trim and place 700 g (1 lb 7 oz) raw beetroot, thickly sliced, on a nonstick roasting tray. Drizzle over 4 tablespoons vegetable oil and sprinkle over 2 teaspoons each ground cumin, ground coriander and chilli powder and 1 teaspoon ground cinnamon. Season well with salt and pepper. Toss to mix well and roast in a preheated oven, 200°C (400°F), Gas Mark 6, for 45–50 minutes or until tender. Remove from the oven, scatter over a small handful of chopped coriander leaves, squeeze over the juice of 1 lime and serve.

cumin potatoes

Serves **4**
Preparation time **20 minutes**
Cooking time **5–7 minutes**

4 tablespoons **sunflower oil**
1 teaspoon **black mustard seeds**
3 teaspoons **cumin seeds**
8–10 **fresh curry leaves**
2 teaspoons **ground cumin**
2 teaspoons **ground coriander**
1 teaspoon **ground turmeric**
500 g (1 lb) **potatoes**, boiled and cut into 2.5 cm (1 inch) cubes
4 tablespoons chopped **coriander leaves**
squeeze of **lime juice**
salt

Heat the oil in a large nonstick wok or frying pan. Add the mustard seeds, cumin seeds and curry leaves.

Stir-fry for 1–2 minutes and then add the ground spices and potatoes. Season well with salt and stir-fry over a high heat for 4–5 minutes.

Remove from the heat, stir in the chopped coriander and add lime juice to taste. Serve immediately.

For spicy potato tortilla wraps, make the Cumin Potatoes as above. Heat 8 tortillas according to the packet instructions and roughly shred ½ iceberg lettuce. Divide the potatoes between the tortillas and top with the lettuce. Drizzle with 75 ml (3 fl oz) natural yogurt, lightly whisked, and roll up.

bengali egg & potato curry

Serves 4
Preparation time **30 minutes**
Cooking time **25–30 minutes**

2 tablespoons **sunflower oil**
1 tablespoon **black mustard seeds**
2 **garlic cloves**, crushed
2 **dried red chillies**
10 **fresh curry leaves**
1 **onion**, thinly sliced
1 teaspoon **chilli powder**
1 tablespoon **ground coriander**
1 tablespoon **cumin seeds**
½ teaspoon **ground turmeric**
200 g (7 oz) canned **chopped tomatoes**
1 teaspoon **sugar**
400 ml (14 fl oz) **coconut milk**
6 **eggs**, hard-boiled, shelled and halved lengthways
2 **potatoes**, boiled and cut into bite-sized pieces
salt
finely chopped **mint leaves**, to garnish

Heat the oil in a large nonstick wok or frying pan, then add the mustard seeds. When they start to pop, add the garlic, chillies and curry leaves and fry for 1 minute. Add the onion and cook, stirring constantly, for 5–6 minutes.

Stir in the chilli powder, coriander, cumin seeds and turmeric, then stir in the tomatoes and sugar. Bring to the boil, reduce the heat and simmer for 8–10 minutes, stirring often.

Add the coconut milk and stir, then add the eggs and potatoes. Cook gently for 8–10 minutes until the sauce has thickened. Season with salt and serve immediately, garnished with chopped mint leaves.

For Bengali prawn & egg curry, proceed as above, adding 16 raw tiger prawns, peeled and deveined, to the curry about 6 minutes before the end of cooking.

spiced potatoes & pomegranate

Serves **4**
Preparation time **10 minutes**
Cooking time **10–15 minutes**

500 g (1 lb) **potatoes**, cut into
   2.5 cm (1 inch) cubes
4 tablespoons **sunflower oil**
1–2 teaspoons **black mustard
seeds**
2 teaspoons **nigella seeds**
1 teaspoon **Kashmiri chilli
powder**
4 teaspoons **cumin seeds**
2 teaspoons **sesame seeds**
8–10 **fresh curry leaves**
2 teaspoons **ground cumin**
2 teaspoons **ground
coriander**
1 teaspoon **ground turmeric**
6 tablespoons chopped
   coriander leaves
4 tablespoons **pomegranate
seeds**
squeeze of **lemon juice**
salt and **pepper**

Boil the potatoes in a large saucepan of lightly salted water for 6–8 minutes or until only just tender. Drain and set aside.

Heat the oil in a large nonstick wok or frying pan over a medium-high heat. Add the mustard seeds, nigella seeds, chilli powder, cumin seeds, sesame seeds and curry leaves and stir-fry for 20–30 seconds.

Add the ground spices and potatoes. Season well with salt and pepper, then stir-fry briskly over a high heat for 4–5 minutes.

Remove from the heat and stir in the chopped coriander and pomegranate seeds. Squeeze over the lemon juice before serving hot.

For creamy baby new potato curry, heat 2 tablespoons vegetable oil in a large nonstick wok over a medium-high heat. Add 4 chopped shallots and stir-fry for 2–3 minutes. Sprinkle over 1 teaspoon each black mustard, cumin, and nigella seeds; ground cumin, coriander and turmeric; and chilli powder and stir-fry for a further 1 minute until fragrant. Add 400 g (13 oz) halved baby new potatoes, 1 crushed garlic clove, a 400 g (13 oz) can chopped tomatoes, 1 teaspoon sugar and 300 ml (½ pint) water and bring to the boil. Reduce the heat to low and simmer, uncovered, for 15–20 minutes. Stir in 200 ml (7 fl oz) double cream and simmer gently for 5 minutes or until the potatoes are tender. Season well with salt and pepper. Remove from the heat and garnish with coriander before serving.

spiced stir-fry okra

Serves **4**
Preparation time **10 minutes**
Cooking time **10–15 minutes**

4 tablespoons **vegetable oil**
1 teaspoon **black mustard seeds**
2 teaspoons **cumin seeds**
2 **onions**, halved and sliced
2 teaspoons **ginger paste**
2 teaspoons **garlic paste**
2 **green chillies**, finely sliced
1 teaspoon **ground coriander**
400 g (13 oz) **okra,** trimmed and cut diagonally into 1 cm (½ inch) thick slices
2 **tomatoes**, roughly chopped
salt

Heat the oil in a wide nonstick frying pan over a high heat and add the black mustard seeds. Once they start to pop (a matter of a few seconds), add the cumin seeds, onions, ginger paste, garlic paste, chillies and coriander. Stir-fry for 1–2 minutes, then add the okra and stir-fry in the mixture for 3–4 minutes.

Stir in the tomatoes, season with salt and continue to stir-fry over a high heat for 4–5 minutes or until the okra is just tender.

Remove from the heat and serve immediately, with Jeera Chapattis (see below) and the raita of your choice, if liked.

For jeera chapattis, to serve as an accompaniment, put 250 g (8 oz) chapatti flour in a mixing bowl with 1 teaspoon salt and 2 teaspoons cumin seeds. Drizzle over 4 tablespoons melted ghee and 150 ml (¼ pint) warm water. Knead in the bowl with your hands until the dough is smooth and elastic, then turn out on to a lightly floured surface and knead for another 1–2 minutes. Divide the dough into 8 portions and form each one into a smooth ball. Roll out each ball into a thin disc on a lightly floured surface until about 20 cm (8 inches) in diameter. If it begins to stick, sprinkle over some more flour. Place a large, flat, nonstick frying pan over a medium-high heat and when hot add a chapatti and cook for 2–3 minutes, turning halfway through and pressing it down with a spatula to cook evenly. It will get lightly browned in places and should look dry. Transfer to a plate and cover with foil and a clean tea towel to keep warm while you cook the remaining chapattis. Serve immediately.

spiced cabbage stir-fry

Serves **4**
Preparation time **10 minutes**
Cooking time **8–10 minutes**

3 tablespoons **vegetable oil**
1 teaspoon **mustard seeds**
1 teaspoon **nigella seeds**
1 teaspoon **cumin seeds**
2 **dried red chillies**
1½ teaspoon finely chopped
  fresh root ginger
10–12 **fresh curry leaves**
1 **white** or **green cabbage**,
  halved, cored and finely
  shredded
½ teaspoon **ground turmeric**
50 g (2 oz) **roasted peanuts**,
  roughly chopped
50 g (2 oz) freshly grated
  coconut
juice of ½ **lime**
salt and **pepper**

Heat the oil in a large nonstick frying pan. Add the mustard, nigella and cumin seeds and stir-fry for 20–30 seconds. Add the chillies, ginger and curry leaves, and stir-fry for a further 10 seconds.

Add the cabbage and turmeric and stir-fry for 6–8 minutes or until the cabbage is lightly browned and just tender (with a slight crispness to it).

Stir in the peanuts, coconut and lime juice. Season well with salt and pepper and serve immediately.

For spiced cabbage & carrot slaw, place ½ finely shredded cabbage in a mixing bowl with 2 coarsely grated carrots, 1 very thinly sliced red onion and a small handful each chopped mint and coriander leaves. Whisk together 8 tablespoons mayonnaise, the juice of 2 limes and 1 teaspoon each toasted cumin seeds, chilli powder and clear honey. Season well and pour into the cabbage mixture. Toss to mix well and serve.

spinach & tomato dhal

Serves **4**
Preparation time **10 minutes**
Cooking time **about 1 hour**

250 g (8 oz) **dried red split
  lentils**, rinsed and drained
½ teaspoon **ground turmeric**
2 **green chillies**, deseeded
  and chopped
2 teaspoons grated **fresh root
  ginger**
1 litre (1¾ pints) **water**
400 g (13 oz) can **chopped
  tomatoes**
250 g (8 oz) **baby spinach
  leaves**
salt

Spiced oil
1 tablespoon **sunflower oil**
1 **shallot**, thinly sliced
12 **fresh curry leaves**
1 teaspoon **black mustard
  seeds**
1 teaspoon **cumin seeds**
1 **dried red chilli**, broken into
  small pieces

Place the lentils in a large saucepan with the turmeric, chillies, ginger and measurement water. Bring to the boil, then reduce the heat and simmer, uncovered, for 40 minutes or until the lentils have broken down and the mixture has thickened.

Add the tomatoes and cook for a further 10 minutes or until thickened. Stir in the spinach and cook for 2–3 minutes until wilted.

Prepare the spiced oil. Heat the oil in a small frying pan, add the shallot and cook over a medium-high heat, stirring, for 2–3 minutes until golden brown. Add all the remaining ingredients and cook, stirring constantly, for 1–2 minutes until the seeds start to pop.

Season with salt to taste. Serve in warmed bowls with the spiced oil spooned over, with naan breads or steamed basmati rice, if liked.

For coconut & spinach dhal, follow the above recipe, replacing the canned chopped tomatoes with 200 ml (7 fl oz) can coconut milk and 4 chopped fresh tomatoes. Serve the dhal with naan breads.

red lentil curry & spiced oil

Serves **4**
Preparation time **10 minutes**
Cooking time **15–20 minutes**

200 g (7 oz) **dried red split lentils**, rinsed and drained
1 litre (1¾ pints) boiling **water**
1 teaspoon **ground turmeric**
1 teaspoon **ground coriander**
1 teaspoon **ground cumin**
2 **green chillies**, split lengthways
1 teaspoon **ginger paste**
2 **tomatoes**, deseeded and chopped
large handful of finely chopped **coriander** (stalks and leaves)
salt

Spiced oil
3 tablespoons **vegetable oil**
1 teaspoon **black mustard seeds**
2 teaspoons **cumin seeds**
10 **fresh curry leaves**
4 **garlic cloves**, thinly sliced
1 **dried red chilli**

To serve
rice
pickles

Place the lentils in a wide saucepan, pour over the measurement boiling water and bring to the boil over a high heat, skimming off foam that comes to the surface.

Reduce the heat to medium and add the turmeric, ground coriander, ground cumin, green chillies and ginger paste. Cook for 15–20 minutes, whisking occasionally, until thickened and tender.

Meanwhile, make the spiced oil. Heat the oil in a small nonstick saucepan over a medium-high heat, add the mustard and cumin seeds, curry leaves, garlic and dried red chilli and stir-fry for 1 minute.

Stir the spiced oil into the lentil mixture with the tomatoes. Season with salt and scatter with chopped coriander. Serve with rice and pickles of your choice.

For quick cauliflower & carrot pickle, to serve as an accompaniment, combine 3 tablespoons golden caster sugar and 175 ml (6 fl oz) cider vinegar in a small pan over a low heat and stir. When the sugar has dissolved, turn off the heat. Pour 125 ml (4 fl oz) vegetable oil into a large pan over a medium heat. Add 1 teaspoon each grated garlic and fresh root ginger and stir for 30 seconds. Add 400 g (13 oz) small cauliflower florets and 4 sliced carrots. Stir and cook for 1 minute or until the vegetables are coated with oil and still crisp. Reduce the heat to low and add 2 tablespoons crushed brown mustard seeds, 2 teaspoons each paprika and salt, 1 teaspoon chilli powder and ½ teaspoon garam masala. Stir for 1–2 minutes, then pour in the sugar-vinegar mixture and stir. Take off the heat and allow to cool. Spoon into sterilized jars, with the juices, and refrigerate (it will keep for 3–4 weeks).

bengali cholar dhal

Serves **4**
Preparation time **15 minutes**
Cooking time **35–40 minutes**

250 g (8 oz) **dried Bengal
gram (chickpeas)** or **dried
yellow split peas**, rinsed
and drained
900 ml (1½ pints) **water**
6 tablespoons **ghee**
1 small **onion**, very finely diced
2 **green chillies**, slit
lengthways
1 tablespoon **ground
coriander**
1 teaspoon **ground cumin**
2 **dried bay leaves**
1 teaspoon **hot chilli powder**
1 teaspoon **ground turmeric**
2 **dried red chillies**
2 **garlic cloves**, very thinly
sliced
2 teaspoons grated **fresh root
ginger**
1 tablespoon **raisins**
2 teaspoons **salt**
2 tablespoons lightly toasted
desiccated coconut,
to garnish

Place the Bengal gram or split peas and measurement water in a pan, stir well and bring to the boil. Skim off any foam that comes to the surface. Cover and reduce the heat. Simmer, stirring regularly, for 35–40 minutes, or until the Bengal gram or split peas are just tender, adding more water if necessary. Remove from the heat and whisk to break them down. Set aside and keep warm.

Meanwhile, heat the ghee in a nonstick frying pan over a medium heat. Add the onion and stir-fry for 4–5 minutes. Add the green chillies, coriander, cumin, bay leaves, chilli powder, turmeric, dried red chillies, garlic and ginger and stir-fry for 1–2 minutes. Add the raisins and stir and cook for 30 seconds.

Pour over the Bengal gram or split peas. Stir in the salt, mix well and heat before serving, garnished with the coconut. Serve with Tomato & Coriander Rice (see below).

For tomato & coriander rice, to serve as an accompaniment, heat 2 tablespoons vegetable oil in a heavy saucepan over a medium heat and fry 4 finely sliced shallots, 2 finely chopped garlic cloves and 2 teaspoons cumin seeds for 4–5 minutes until soft and fragrant. Add 4 finely chopped tomatoes and 275 g (9 oz) washed, drained basmati rice and stir-fry for 2–3 minutes. Season with salt and pepper, pour over 600 ml (1 pint) water and bring to the boil. Cover the pan tightly, reduce the heat to low and cook for 10–12 minutes. Remove from the heat and leave to stand, covered, for 10 minutes. When ready to serve, uncover and fluff up the grains of rice with a fork. Stir in 4 tablespoons chopped coriander. Serve immediately.

masala dhal with sweet potato

Serves **4**
Preparation time **15 minutes**
Cooking time **50 minutes**

3 tablespoons **vegetable oil**
2 **onions**, chopped
2 **garlic cloves**, crushed
½ teaspoon **dried chilli flakes**
1.5 cm (¾ inch) piece of **fresh root ginger**, grated
2 teaspoons **garam masala**
½ teaspoon **ground turmeric**
250 g (8 oz) **dried yellow split peas**, rinsed and drained
200 g (7 oz) can **chopped tomatoes**
1 litre (1¾ pints) **vegetable stock**
500 g (1 lb) **sweet potatoes**, scrubbed and cut into small chunks
200 g (7 oz) **spinach**
salt

Heat the oil in a saucepan and fry the onions for 5 minutes. Add the garlic, chilli flakes, ginger, garam masala and turmeric and cook, stirring, for 2 minutes.

Add the split peas, tomatoes and 750 ml (1¼ pints) of the stock and bring to the boil. Reduce the heat, cover and cook gently for 20 minutes until the peas have started to soften. Add more stock if the mixture runs dry.

Stir in the sweet potatoes, re-cover and cook for a further 20 minutes until the potatoes and peas are tender, adding more stock if necessary to keep the dahl juicy.

Tip the spinach into the pan and stir until wilted. Add a little salt to taste and serve with Spiced Naan Breads (see below) and mango chutney.

For homemade spiced naan breads, to serve as an accompaniment, mix 250 g (8 oz) strong white flour and 1 teaspoon each crushed coriander seeds, crushed cumin seeds, salt and fast-action dried yeast in a bowl. Add 2 tablespoons natural yogurt and 125 ml (4 fl oz) warm milk and mix with a round-bladed knife to a soft dough, adding a dash more water if it feels dry. Knead on a lightly floured surface for 10 minutes (or use a free-standing mixer with a dough hook attachment, kneading for 5 minutes). Turn into a bowl, cover with clingfilm and leave to rise for about 1 hour until it has doubled in size. Turn out on to a floured surface and divide into 4 equal pieces. Roll out each into a tear shape about 22 cm (8½ inches) long. Heat a flat griddle or dry frying pan until hot and cook for 2–3 minutes on each side until puffed and lightly browned.

spiced chickpea with spinach

Serves **4**
Preparation time **5 minutes**
Cooking time **15–20 minutes**

4 tablespoons **vegetable oil**
2 teaspoons **cumin seeds**
2 **onions,** chopped
1 teaspoon **garlic paste**
1 teaspoon **ginger paste**
1 **green chilli**, deseeded and
   thinly sliced
1½ teaspoons **amchoor**
1½ teaspoon **garam masala**
½ teaspoon **ground turmeric**
1 teaspoon **Kashmiri chilli
   powder** or **mild chilli powder**
500 g (1 lb) **passata with
   onion and garlic**
2 x 400 g (13 oz) cans
   chickpeas, drained
200 g (7 oz) **baby spinach
   leaves**
salt
flatbreads, to serve

Heat the oil in a large, wide nonstick frying pan over a medium-high heat. Add the cumin seeds and stir for 20–30 seconds, then add the onions, garlic paste, ginger paste and chilli and stir-fry for 3–4 minutes.

Stir in the amchoor, garam masala, turmeric, chilli powder and passata and cook over a high heat, stirring often, for 6–8 minutes.

Add the chickpeas and spinach, stir and cook for 3–4 minutes or until the spinach has wilted.

Season well with salt and serve immediately with warmed flatbreads.

For spinach & chickpea pilau, heat 2 tablespoons vegetable oil in a heavy-based saucepan over a medium heat and fry 1 finely sliced onion, 3 finely chopped garlic cloves and 2 teaspoons mild curry powder for 4–5 minutes. Add a 400 g (13 oz) can chickpeas, drained, 200 g (7 oz) finely chopped spinach and 275 g (9 oz) washed, drained basmati rice and stir-fry for 2–3 minutes. Season well with salt and pepper and pour over 600 ml (1 pint) water. Bring to the boil, cover the pan tightly, reduce the heat to low and cook for 10–12 minutes. Remove from the heat and leave to stand, covered, for 10 minutes. When ready to serve, uncover and fluff up the grains of rice with a fork.

paneer curry

Serves **4**
Preparation time **15 minutes**
Cooking time **25–30 minutes**

1 tablespoon **groundnut oil**
8 **shallots**, finely chopped
2 tablespoons **curry powder**
4 **ripe plum tomatoes**,
   roughly chopped
2 teaspoons finely grated
   garlic
2 **fresh red chillies**, deseeded
   and finely sliced
2 tablespoons **tomato purée**
1 teaspoon **palm sugar** or
   brown sugar
150 ml (¼ pint) **water**
200 ml (7 fl oz) **passata**
500 g (1 lb) **paneer cheese**,
   cubed
200 g (7 oz) **fresh** or **frozen**
   peas
6 tablespoons finely chopped
   coriander leaves
salt and **pepper**

Heat the oil in a large nonstick wok over a medium-high heat. Add the shallots and stir-fry for 2–3 minutes. Sprinkle over the curry powder and stir-fry for a further 1 minute until fragrant.

Add the tomatoes, garlic, chillies, tomato purée, sugar and measurement water and bring to the boil. Reduce the heat to low and simmer, uncovered, for 15–20 minutes.

Stir in the passata, paneer and peas and simmer gently for 5 minutes or until the paneer is heated through and the peas are cooked. Season to taste, remove from the heat and stir in most of the chopped coriander just before serving. Serve scattered with the remaining coriander.

For spicy paneer bruschetta, finely grate 300 g (10 oz) paneer cheese into a bowl. Add 4 finely diced shallots, ½ peeled, deseeded and finely diced cucumber, 1 finely chopped green chilli, a small handful of finely chopped coriander leaves, 2 tablespoons light olive oil and the juice of 2 limes. Season to taste and toss to mix. Lightly toast 12 thick slices of ciabatta bread and place on a serving plate. Spoon the paneer mixture on to the toast and serve immediately.

red kidney bean curry

Serves **4**
Preparation time **10 minutes**
Cooking time **15–18 minutes**

2 tablespoons **vegetable oil**
2 teaspoons **cumin seeds**
1 **onion,** finely chopped
2 teaspoons **ginger paste**
3 teaspoons **garlic paste**
2 **green chillies**, finely chopped
2 large **tomatoes**, roughly chopped
2 teaspoons **ground coriander**
1 teaspoon **ground cumin**
1¼ teaspoon **ground turmeric**
1 teaspoon **garam masala**
2 x 400 g (13 oz) cans **red kidney beans**, drained and rinsed
1 teaspoon **palm sugar**
300 ml (½ pint) warm **water**
100 ml (3½ fl oz) **double cream**
salt
4 tablespoons finely chopped **coriander leaves**, to garnish
4 tablespoons whisked **natural yogurt**, to serve

Heat the oil in a deep pan and add the cumin seeds. When they stop sizzling (a matter of a few seconds), add the onion, ginger and garlic pastes, chillies, tomatoes, ground coriander, cumin, turmeric and garam masala and stir-fry over a medium heat for 3–4 minutes.

Add the red kidney beans, palm sugar, measurement water and cream. Season well with salt and cook over a high heat for 10–12 minutes, stirring often, or until thickened.

Remove from the heat, garnish with the chopped coriander and serve with a dollop of yogurt.

For red kidney bean biryani, heat 2 tablespoons vegetable oil in a heavy saucepan over a medium heat. Fry 1 finely chopped red onion, 2 finely chopped shallots, 2 finely chopped garlic cloves and 2 teaspoons grated fresh root ginger for 1–2 minutes. Add 1 tablespoon biryani paste, a 400 g (13 oz) can red kidney beans in chilli sauce, 2 chopped tomatoes and 275 g (9 oz) washed, drained basmati rice and stir-fry for 2–3 minutes. Season well with salt and pepper, pour over 600 ml (1 pint) water and bring to the boil. Cover the pan tightly, reduce the heat to low and cook for 10–12 minutes. Remove from the heat and leave to stand, covered, for 10 minutes. When ready to serve, uncover and fluff up the grains of rice with a fork. Stir in a small handful of chopped mint and serve immediately.

south indian vegetable stew

Serves **4**
Preparation time **15 minutes**
Cooking time **20–25 minutes**

1 tablespoon **groundnut oil**
6 **shallots**, halved and thinly
   sliced
2 teaspoons **black mustard
   seeds**
8–10 **fresh curry leaves**
1 **green chilli**, thinly sliced
2 teaspoons finely grated
   fresh root ginger
1 teaspoon **ground turmeric**
2 teaspoons **ground cumin**
6 **black peppercorns**
2 **carrots**, cut into thick batons
1 **courgette**, cut into thick
   batons
200 g (7 oz) **French beans**,
   trimmed
1 **potato**, cut into thin batons
400 ml (14 fl oz) **reduced-fat
   coconut milk**
400 ml (14 fl oz) **vegetable
   stock**
2 tablespoons **lemon juice**
salt and **pepper**

Heat the oil in a large frying pan over a medium heat.
Add the shallots and stir-fry for 4–5 minutes. Add the
mustard seeds, curry leaves, chilli, ginger, turmeric,
cumin and peppercorns and stir-fry for a further
1–2 minutes until fragrant.

Add the carrots, courgette, beans and potato to the pan.
Pour in the coconut milk and stock and bring to the boil.
Reduce the heat to low, cover and simmer gently for
12–15 minutes until the vegetables are tender.

Season to taste, remove from the heat and drizzle over
the lemon juice just before serving.

For spicy tomato, vegetable & coconut curry, follow
the above recipe, replacing the turmeric, cumin and
black peppercorns with 2 tablespoons hot curry powder,
and the vegetable stock with 400 ml (14 fl oz) passata.
Serve with steamed white rice.

tandoori broccoli

Serves **4**
Preparation time **10 minutes**
Cooking time **4–5 minutes**

1 head **broccoli**, cut into large
　florets
200 ml (7 fl oz) **Greek yogurt**
1 tablespoon finely chopped
　lemon grass or **lemon**
　grass paste
finely grated zest and juice of
　1 lime
50 g (2 oz) **cream cheese**
1 teaspoon **green chilli paste**
1 teaspoon **garlic paste**
1 teaspoon **ginger paste**
1 teaspoon **tandoori paste**
salt and **pepper**

Blanch the broccoli in a pan of lightly salted boiling
water for 1 minute. Drain, rinse under cold running
water, drain again and pat dry with kitchen paper.

Put the remaining ingredients in a large mixing bowl
and, using a whisk, mix until smooth. Add the broccoli
to this mixture and toss to coat evenly.

Thread the broccoli on to 8 metal skewers and place
under a preheated medium-hot grill. Cook for 3–4 minutes,
turning once, until the coating begins to brown and the
broccoli is just cooked through. Remove from the grill
and serve immediately.

For broccoli & mixed pepper curry, heat 2 tablespoons
vegetable oil in a large nonstick frying pan over a
medium heat. Add 6 sliced spring onions and stir-fry
for 2–3 minutes. Add 2 teaspoons each of grated garlic,
grated fresh root ginger and hot curry powder and
stir-fry for 20–30 seconds until fragrant. Add 500 g
(1 lb) broccoli florets and 1 red pepper and 1 yellow
pepper, cored, deseeded and sliced and stir-fry for
a further 2–3 minutes. Stir in a 400 g (13 oz) can
chopped tomatoes and 200 ml (7 fl oz) vegetable stock
and bring to the boil. Cover, reduce the heat to medium
and simmer for 10 minutes, stirring occasionally until
just tender. Remove from the heat. To serve, drizzle with
4 tablespoons whisked natural yogurt and garnish with
chopped mint. Serve hot with steamed rice.

spiced semolina with vegetables

Serves **4**
Preparation time **10 minutes**
Cooking time **about**
  15 minutes

200 g (7 oz) **coarse semolina**
2 tablespoons **vegetable oil**
25 g (1 oz) **butter**
1 teaspoon **black mustard**
  seeds
1 teaspoon **cumin seeds**
1 **dried red chilli**
10–12 **fresh curry leaves**
1 **red onion**, chopped
2 tablespoons toasted
  cashew nuts
100 g (3½ oz) **frozen peas**
600 ml (1 pint) boiling
  vegetable stock
juice of ½ **lemon**
salt and **pepper**

To garnish
2 tablespoons freshly grated
  coconut
small handful of chopped
  coriander leaves

Heat a wide nonstick pan over a medium heat and add
the semolina. Dry-fry for 1–2 minutes, transfer to a bowl
or plate and set aside.

Put the oil and butter in the frying pan and place over
a high heat. Add the mustard seeds, cumin seeds, dried
chilli and curry leaves. When the mustard seeds start to
pop (a matter of a few seconds), add the onion and stir-
fry for 1–2 minutes.

Add the cashew nuts, peas, semolina and stock, season
well with salt and pepper and cook over a gentle heat
for 10–12 minutes, stirring constantly, until all the liquid
is absorbed. Remove from the heat and stir in the
lemon juice.

Garnish with the coconut and coriander before serving
with Yogurt Pachadi, if liked (see below).

For yogurt pachadi, to serve as an accompaniment,
put 1 finely diced cucumber, 2 finely chopped tomatoes,
2 teaspoons sugar and 5 tablespoons finely chopped
coriander leaves in a bowl and season with sea salt.
In a separate bowl, whisk 400 ml (13 fl oz) natural
yogurt until smooth, then pour over the cucumber
mixture and toss to coat well. Transfer to a shallow
serving bowl. Heat 2 tablespoons vegetable oil in
a small frying pan until hot. Add 1 teaspoon black
mustard seeds and 2 teaspoons cumin seeds, stir-fry
for 30–40 seconds, remove from the heat and drizzle
the spiced oil over the cucumber mixture. Sprinkle over
1 teaspoon paprika and serve.

paneer korma

Serves **4**
Preparation time **20 minutes**
Cooking time **25–30 minutes**

2 tablespoons s**unflower oil**
8 **shallots**, finely chopped
1 teaspoon **ground cumin**
1 teaspoon **ground coriander**
1 teaspoon **ground turmeric**
1 teaspoon **chilli powder**
1 teaspoon **garam masala**
4 **ripe plum tomatoes**,
  roughly chopped
2 teaspoons crushed **garlic**
2 **red chillies**, deseeded and
  finely sliced
2 tablespoons **tomato purée**
1 teaspoon **sugar**
150 ml (¼ pint) **water**
200 ml (7 fl oz) **single cream**
450 g (14½ oz) **paneer
  cheese**, cut into bite-sized
  pieces
200 g (7 oz) **frozen peas**
small handful of finely chopped
  coriander leaves
salt and **pepper**
Crisp Poppadums (see page
  190), to serve

Heat the oil in a large nonstick wok or frying pan, add the shallots and stir-fry for 2–3 minutes. Add the ground spices and stir-fry for 1 minute.

Add the tomatoes, garlic, chillies, tomato purée, sugar and measurement water and bring to the boil. Reduce the heat and simmer, uncovered, for 15–20 minutes.

Stir in the cream, paneer and peas and simmer gently for 5 minutes or until the paneer is heated through and the peas are cooked.

Season well, remove from the heat and stir in the chopped coriander just before serving. Serve immediately piled on to Crisp Poppadums.

For royal paneer korma pilau, follow the above recipe, at the same time cooking 250 g (8 oz) basmati rice according to the packet instructions. Add the rice to the cooked korma, forking the ingredients together carefully. Top with crispy fried onions.

kashmiri pumpkin curry

Serves **4**
Preparation time **20 minutes**
Cooking time **25 minutes**

2 **onions**, quartered
2 **garlic cloves**
3.5 cm (1½ inch) piece of
  fresh root ginger, sliced
1 large **red chilli**, halved and
  deseeded
1 teaspoon **cumin seeds,**
  roughly crushed
1 teaspoon **coriander seeds**,
  roughly crushed
5 **green cardamom pods**,
  crushed
1.4 kg (2¾ lb) **pumpkin**,
  peeled and deseeded
15 g (½ oz) **butter**
2 tablespoons **sunflower oil**
1 teaspoon **ground turmeric**
1 teaspoon **paprika**
1 **cinnamon stick**, halved
450 ml (¾ pint) **vegetable
  stock**
150 ml (¼ pint) **double cream**
50 g (2 oz) **pistachio nuts**,
  roughly chopped
1 small bunch of **coriander**,
  torn
salt and **pepper**

Place the onions, garlic, ginger and chilli in a food processor and process until finely chopped, or finely chop by hand. Mix with the crushed cumin seeds, coriander seeds and cardamom pods.

Slice the pumpkin into 2.5 cm (1 inch) wedges, then cut the wedges in half. Melt the butter with the oil in a large frying pan and fry the pumpkin for 5 minutes until lightly browned. Push the pumpkin to one side of the pan, add the onion mixture and fry for about 5 minutes until beginning to colour.

Add the turmeric, paprika and cinnamon to the pan and cook briefly, then stir in the stock. Season to taste with salt and pepper and bring to the boil. Reduce the heat, cover and simmer for 10 minutes or until the pumpkin is just cooked.

Stir in half the cream, half the pistachios and half the coriander leaves and gently heat through. Drizzle with the remaining cream and sprinkle with the remaining pistachios and coriander. Serve with rice and naan breads.

For Kashmiri aubergine curry, make the curry as above using 2 large aubergines, cut into 3.5 cm (1½ inch) cubes, in place of the pumpkin and adding 200 g (7 oz) French beans, topped and tailed, then halved, with the stock. Finish as above with the cream and coriander but using 50 g (2 oz) roughly chopped blanched almonds instead of the pistachios.

mushroom curry

Serves **4**
Preparation time **20 minutes**
Cooking time **about 35 minutes**

2 tablespoons **vegetable oil**
1 teaspoon **cumin seeds**
1 teaspoon **coriander seeds**
1 **onion**, finely chopped
2 teaspoons **ground coriander**
1 teaspoon **ground cumin**
6 **black peppercorns**
½ teaspoon **ground cardamom**
1 teaspoon **ground turmeric**
1 tablespoon **tandoori spice mix**
1 **red chilli**, finely chopped
2 **garlic cloves**, crushed
2 teaspoons grated **fresh root ginger**
2 x 400 g (13 oz) cans **chopped tomatoes**
600 g (1 lb 3½ oz) **chestnut** or **button mushrooms**, halved or thickly sliced
2 teaspoons **salt**
200 g (7 oz) **frozen peas**
4 tablespoons roughly chopped **coriander leaves**
6 tablespoons **double cream**

Heat the oil in a large saucepan over a medium heat. Add the cumin and coriander seeds and cook for 1 minute or until sizzling. Add the onion, ground coriander, cumin, peppercorns, cardamom, turmeric, tandoori spice mix, chilli, garlic and ginger. Cook, stirring, for 2–3 minutes or until the onion is soft and the mixture is aromatic.

Add the tomatoes, mushrooms and salt. Stir until well combined, then bring to the boil. Reduce the heat to low and cook, uncovered, for 25 minutes. Add the peas and stir to mix well. Cook for 4–5 minutes or until piping hot.

Remove from the heat, scatter over the coriander leaves and drizzle over the cream. Stir to mix well. Serve with chapattis or basmati rice.

For mushroom pilau, heat 3 tablespoons ghee in a heavy-based saucepan over a high heat. Add 300 g (10 oz) sliced button mushrooms and stir-fry for 6–8 minutes. Add 1 cinnamon stick, 2 teaspoons cumin seeds, 4 cloves, 4 lightly crushed green cardamom pods, 8–10 black peppercorns and 4 tablespoons shop-bought crispy fried onions. Stir-fry for 2–3 minutes, then add 200 g (7 oz) peas and stir-fry for a further 2–3 minutes. Add 275 g (9 oz) washed, drained basmati rice and stir for 1 minute or so until the grains are well coated. Pour over 600 ml (1 pint) vegetable stock. Season well with salt and pepper and bring to the boil. Cover the pan tightly, reduce the heat to low and cook for 10–12 minutes. Remove from the heat and leave to stand, covered, for 10–15 minutes. Uncover and fluff up the grains of rice with a fork. Serve immediately.

mushroom & cashew nut curry

Serves **4**
Preparation time **10 minutes**
Cooking time **12–15 minutes**

2 tablespoons **vegetable oil**
1 **onion**, chopped
1 teaspoon **garlic paste**
1 teaspoon **ginger paste**
500 g (1 lb) **mixed open** and
    closed cup mushrooms,
    roughly chopped or sliced
100 g (3½ oz) **frozen peas**
100 g (3½ oz) **roasted**
    cashew nuts
4 tablespoons **korma curry**
    paste
400 ml (14 fl oz) **coconut milk**
squeeze of **lemon juice**
pinch of **sugar**
salt and **pepper**

Heat the oil in a frying pan, add the onion and sauté over a medium heat for 2–3 minutes.

Add the garlic paste, ginger paste and mushrooms to the pan and sauté for 5–6 minutes or until the mushrooms are lightly browned.

Stir in the peas, cashew nuts, korma curry paste, coconut milk, lemon juice and sugar. Bring to the boil, then simmer, uncovered, for 5–6 minutes or until the sauce has thickened slightly.

Season to taste and serve with rice or Saffron & Cardamom Pilau (see page 200), if liked.

For mushroom & tomato curry, heat 3 tablespoons vegetable oil in a large nonstick wok over a high heat. Add 500 g (1 lb) halved chestnut mushrooms and stir-fry for 4–5 minutes. Add 1 finely chopped onion, 4 crushed garlic cloves and 2 teaspoons grated fresh root ginger and stir-fry for 3–4 minutes. Stir in 4 finely chopped tomatoes and 100 ml (3½ fl oz) double cream. Stir and cook for 3–4 minutes until piping hot. Season well with salt and pepper. Stir in a small handful of finely chopped coriander, and serve immediately.

side dishes

gujarati carrot salad

Serves **4**
Preparation time **10 minutes**
Cooking time **under 2
  minutes**

2 large **carrots**, coarsely
  grated or shredded
¼ small **red cabbage**, finely
  shredded
½ **red onion**, halved and very
  thinly sliced
4 tablespoons **vegetable oil**
2 teaspoons **black mustard
  seeds**
1 teaspoon **caster sugar**
1 **garlic clove**, crushed
½ teaspoon **ground cumin**
½ teaspoon **dried chilli flakes**
juice of ½ **orange**
juice of 1 **lemon**
small handful of chopped
  coriander leaves
small handful of chopped **mint
  leaves**
salt and **pepper**

Place the carrots, cabbage and red onion in a wide
salad bowl.

Heat the oil in a small frying pan. When hot, add the
mustard seeds and cook for 30 seconds or until they
start to pop.

Pour over the grated carrot mixture with the sugar,
garlic, cumin, chilli flakes and orange and lemon juice
and season well with salt and pepper. Toss to mix well,
cover and chill until ready to serve.

Scatter over the chopped coriander and mint, toss
and serve.

For carrot & ginger pickle, cut 4 large carrots into
thick batons and place in a saucepan with 2 thickly
sliced onions and 3 red chillies. Add 150 ml (¼ pint)
white wine vinegar and 300 ml (½ pint) water, then
sprinkle in ½ teaspoon ground turmeric and
1 tablespoon sea salt. Bring to the boil and cook for
3–4 minutes. Drain the vegetables and set aside. In a
mini food processor or blender, blend 150 ml (¼ pint)
white wine vinegar, 6 garlic cloves, 1 tablespoon grated
fresh root ginger, 1 tablespoon black mustard seeds,
2 teaspoons coarse chilli powder and 1 tablespoon
sugar to a fairly smooth paste. Season with sea salt,
blend again briefly and transfer to a bowl. Add the
drained vegetables and toss to coat evenly. Pack the
pickle mixture in a sterilized jar and seal with a vinegar-
proof lid. Store in a cool, dark place for 2 weeks before
eating, and refrigerate once opened. It will keep in the
refrigerator for up to 1 month.

potato & bean salad

Serves **4**

Preparation time **10 minutes**

Cooking time **8–10 minutes**

2 **potatoes**, cut into 1 cm
  (½ inch) dice

100 g (3½ oz) **green beans**,
  cut into 2.5 cm (1 inch)
  pieces

400 g (13 oz) can **black-eyed
  beans**, drained and rinsed

4 **spring onions**, thinly sliced

1 **red chilli**, deseeded and
  thinly sliced or finely diced

2 **plum tomatoes**, deseeded
  and finely chopped

small handful of chopped
  coriander leaves

small handful of chopped **mint
  leaves**

salt and **pepper**

Dressing

2 tablespoons **light olive oil**

juice of 1 **lemon**

1 teaspoon **chilli powder**

1 teaspoon **clear honey**

Cook the potatoes in a saucepan of lightly salted
boiling water for 8–10 minutes or until just tender,
adding the green beans for the last 2 minutes of
cooking time.

Drain and place in a serving bowl with the black-eyed
beans, spring onions, chilli, tomatoes and herbs.

Mix all the dressing ingredients together and season
well with salt and pepper. Stir into the salad and toss
to mix well. Serve immediately.

For bean sprout, potato & tomato salad, wash 100 g
(3½ oz) fresh bean sprouts thoroughly in a colander or
large sieve. Blanch in boiling water for 30 seconds, then
drain and rinse again in cold water. Place in a mixing
bowl with 1 cooked, diced potato, 6 finely sliced spring
onions, 2 finely chopped tomatoes and a small handful
each of chopped mint and coriander leaves. In a small
bowl, mix 2 tablespoons light olive oil, the juice of
2 limes, 1 teaspoon ground cumin, 1 teaspoon mild
chilli powder and 1 finely chopped green chilli. Season
well and toss to combine. Leave to stand at room
temperature for 30 minutes before serving.

lime pickle

Makes **1 jar**
Preparation time **20 minutes,
plus maturing**
Cooking time **5 minute**s

10 **limes,** each cut into
6 segments
100 g (3½ oz) **salt**
1 tablespoon **fenugreek
seeds**
1 tablespoon **black mustard
seeds**
1 tablespoon **chilli powder**
1 tablespoon **ground turmeric**
300 ml (½ pint) **vegetable oil**
½ teaspoon **asafoetida
powder**

Put the limes in a sterilized jar and cover with the salt. Dry-fry the fenugreek and mustard seeds in a small frying pan until starting to pop, then leave to cool. Grind them to a powder. Add the ground seeds, chilli powder and turmeric to the limes and mix well.

Heat the oil in a small frying pan until smoking, add the asafoetida and fry for 30 seconds. Pour the oil over the limes and mix well.

Cover the jar with a clean cloth and leave to mature for 10 days in a bright, warm place.

Transfer the pickle to a tightly covered container and store for up to 2 months.

For carrot & lime pickle, use 5 limes and 1 large carrot cut into 1.5 cm (½ inch) pieces. Proceed as above.

stuffed green chilli pickle

Serves **4–6**

Preparation time **30 minutes, plus maturing**

Cooking time **1 minute**

20 **mild green chillies** (such as Serrano)

3 tablespoons **ground coriander**

½–1 tablespoon **fennel seeds**

1 teaspoon **fenugreek seeds**

1 teaspoon **black mustard seeds**

⅛ teaspoons **asafoetida powder**

3 teaspoons **sea salt**

1 teaspoon **amchoor**

½ teaspoon **ground turmeric**

4 tablespoons **mustard oil**

2 tablespoons **white wine vinegar**

Wash and dry the chillies, then cut a vertical slit, lengthways, in each one.

Place the coriander and fennel, fenugreek and mustard seeds in a spice or coffee grinder and grind coarsely. Transfer to a bowl. Add the asafoetida, salt, amchoor and turmeric to the ground spices and mix well.

Heat the oil in a small frying pan until hot, then stir in the spice mixture. Stir-fry for 1 minute and remove from the heat. Add the vinegar and stir to mix well.

Stuff the green chillies with the spice mix and place in a sterilized glass jars. Store the jars in a sunny location (near a kitchen window) for up to 2 days before using. This pickle can be refrigerated for up to 1 month.

For fresh shallot pickle, put 10–12 small shallots, thinly sliced, 2 finely sliced green chillies and 2 finely shredded lime leaves into a non-metallic bowl, then stir in 1 tablespoon each finely grated fresh root ginger, sea salt, sugar and the juice of 2 limes. Stir to mix well, cover and leave to stand at room temperature for 2–3 hours.

cucumber & pomegranate raita

Serves **4**

Preparation time **6–8 minutes**

Cooking time **about 1 minute**

1 **cucumber,** coarsely grated

300 ml (½ pint) **natural yogurt**, whisked

2 tablespoons **vegetable oil**

1 teaspoon **black mustard seeds**

4 **fresh curry leaves**

2 **dried red chillies,** broken in half

2 teaspoons **cumin seeds**

4 tablespoons freshly grated **coconut**

2 tablespoons finely chopped **coriander leaves**

2 tablespoons **pomegranate seeds**

2 tablespoons **toasted peanuts**, roughly chopped

salt and **pepper**

Place the cucumber in a bowl with the yogurt.

Heat the oil in a frying pan and add the mustard seeds, curry leaves, chillies and cumin seeds. Stir-fry for 1 minute.

Remove from the heat, stir into the cucumber mixture with the coconut and chopped coriander and season well with salt and pepper. Stir to mix well and transfer to a serving bowl.

Scatter over the pomegranate seeds and chopped peanut, cover and chill until ready to serve.

For fruity pomegranate & cucumber salad, place 6 tablespoons pomegranate seeds in a bowl with 1 deseeded, roughly chopped cucumber, 1 deseeded, roughly chopped guava, 200 g (7 oz) peeled, stoned lychees and 200 g (7 oz) black seedless grapes. Sprinkle over 1 teaspoon ground cumin and ½ teaspoon chilli powder, the juice of 2 limes and a handful of chopped mint leaves. Season and toss to mix well. Serve chilled or at room temperature.

mango & pineapple raita

Serves **4**

Preparation time **15 minutes**

Cooking time **about 1 minute**

250 ml (8 fl oz) **natural set yogurt**

1 **onion**, finely sliced

1 **tomato**, finely chopped

1 **green chilli**, finely chopped

100 g (3½ oz) **pineapple flesh**, finely diced

100 g (3½ oz) **ripe mango flesh**, finely diced

¼ teaspoon **salt**

2 tablespoons **vegetable oil**

1 teaspoon **black mustard seeds**

4 **fresh curry leaves**

flatbreads, to serve

Place the yogurt in a bowl and whisk until smooth. Add the onion, tomato, chilli, pineapple, mango and salt and stir to mix well.

Heat the oil in a small frying pan and add the mustard seeds and curry leaves. Stir-fry for a few seconds or until the mustard seeds start to pop.

Remove from the heat and pour over the yogurt mixture. Stir to mix gently, then cover and chill until ready to serve. Serve with warmed flatbreads.

For mango, chilli & pineapple salsa, finely dice the flesh of 1 large mango and place in a bowl with 200 g (7 oz) diced pineapple flesh, 1 finely diced red chilli, ½ finely diced red onion, a small handful of chopped coriander leaves, the juice of 2 limes and 1 teaspoon toasted cumin seeds. Season and toss to mix well.

peanut & coconut raita

Serves **4**
Preparation time **10 minutes**
Cooking time **about 5 minutes**

2 tablespoons **vegetable oil**
4 **shallots**, finely chopped
2 **green chillies**, finely chopped
2 teaspoons finely grated **fresh root ginger**
1 teaspoon **black mustard seeds**
4 **fresh curry leaves**
2 **dried red chillies**, broken in half
2 teaspoons **cumin seeds**
275 ml (9 fl oz) **natural set yogurt**, whisked
1 teaspoon **salt**
4 tablespoons freshly grated **coconut**
½ **cucumber**, coarsely grated
2 tablespoons finely chopped **coriander leaves**
4 tablespoons **toasted peanuts**, roughly chopped
flatbreads, to serve

Heat the oil in a frying pan, add the shallots and stir-fry over a gentle heat for 3–4 minutes.

Add the green chillies, ginger, mustard seeds, curry leaves, dried red chillies and cumin seeds. Stir-fry for 1 minute and remove from the heat.

Stir in the yogurt, salt, coconut, cucumber and coriander. Mix well and transfer to a serving bowl. Scatter over the peanuts, cover and chill until ready to serve. Serve with warmed flatbreads.

For chickpea & potato raita, mix 1 tablespoon pepper, 2 teaspoons each sea salt and roughly ground dry-roasted cumin seeds, 1 teaspoon amchoor and 1 teaspoon chilli powder. Add 100 ml (3½ fl oz) whisked natural yogurt and the juice of 1 lemon. Place a 400 g (13 oz) can chickpeas, drained, in a bowl with 3 boiled, cubed potatoes, 2 sliced shallots and ¼ cucumber, deseeded and chopped. Stir in the spiced yogurt mixture and toss to mix well. Cover with clingfilm and chill in the refrigerator for 30 minutes to allow the flavours to develop. Just before serving, toss in a small handful of finely chopped coriander. Mix well and serve.

crispy okra relish

Serves **4**
Preparation time **5 minutes**
Cooking time **about 5
minutes**

6 tablespoons **vegetable oil**
100 g (3½ oz) **okra**, rinsed,
  well dried and cut into 1 cm
  (½ inch) slices
400 ml (14 fl oz) **natural set
  yogurt**
1 teaspoon **sugar**
1 teaspoon **cayenne pepper**
¼ teaspoon **ground turmeric**
1 teaspoon **ground cumin**
1 teaspoon **black mustard
  seeds**
salt and **pepper**
2 tablespoons finely chopped
  coriander leaves, to garnish

Heat 4 tablespoons of the oil in a large frying pan over
a medium heat. When the oil is very hot, add the okra,
toss, and cook for 3–4 minutes, stirring occasionally.
The okra will slowly turn crisp and brown. Drain on
kitchen paper and set aside until ready to serve.

Whisk the yogurt with the sugar in a medium serving
bowl. Sprinkle the cayenne, turmeric and ground cumin
over the top and season well with salt and pepper.

Heat the remaining oil in a small frying pan over a high
heat. When the oil begins to smoke, add the mustard
seeds. After the seeds stop popping, pour the hot oil
directly over the top of the yogurt (this cooks the ground
spices without burning them).

Place the crisp okra on top and garnish with the
chopped coriander just before serving.

For bhindi masala curry, heat 2 tablespoons vegetable
oil in a large nonstick wok or frying pan over a medium
heat. Add 8–10 fresh curry leaves, 2 teaspoons black
mustard seeds and 1 finely diced onion. Stir-fry for
3–4 minutes until fragrant and the onion is starting
to soften, then add 2 teaspoons each ground cumin
and curry powder, 1 teaspoon ground coriander and
1 teaspoon turmeric. Stir-fry for a further 1–2 minutes
until fragrant. Add 3 finely chopped garlic cloves and
500 g (1 lb) thickly sliced okra and increase the heat to
high. Cook, stirring, for 2–3 minutes, then add 2 finely
chopped tomatoes. Season well with salt and pepper,
cover and reduce the heat to low. Cook gently for
10–12 minutes, stirring occasionally, until the okra
is just tender. Remove from the heat and serve.

coriander chutney

Serves **4**

Preparation time **10 minutes**

100 g (3½ oz) finely grated
   fresh coconut (or defrosted
   if frozen)
2 **green chillies**, chopped
50 g (2 oz) **coriander** (leaves
   and stalks), chopped
25 g (1 oz) **mint leaves**,
   chopped
1 teaspoon **ginger paste**
1 teaspoon **garlic paste**
1 teaspoon **caster sugar**
100 ml (3½ fl oz) **natural
   yogurt**
juice of 2 **limes**
salt and **pepper**

Place all the ingredients except the seasoning in a mini
food processor or blender and blend until fairly smooth
(you might want to add a little extra yogurt if very thick).

Season well with salt and pepper, cover and chill until
ready to serve.

For spicy cucumber & tomato wrap, spread
2 tablespoons coriander chutney from the above recipe
on to a warmed chapatti or flatbread. Add ½ chopped
tomato and ¼ deseeded and chopped cucumber with
¼ finely chopped red onion. Scatter over a couple of
mint leaves and a dollop of natural yogurt. Roll up the
chapatti to enclose the filling and serve immediately.

kachumber

Serves **4**

Preparation time **10 minutes**, plus standing

1 **red onion**, finely chopped

4 **ripe tomatoes**, deseeded and finely chopped

1 **cucumber**, finely chopped

1 **green chilli**, deseeded and finely chopped

1 small handful of finely chopped **coriander**

juice of 2 large **limes**

1 tablespoon roughly chopped **roasted peanuts** (optional)

salt and **pepper**

1 **lime** halved, to serve

Put the onion, tomatoes, cucumber, chilli and coriander in a non-metallic bowl and pour over the lime juice. Season well with salt and pepper, cover and allow to stand at room temperature for 10–15 minutes.

Stir to mix well, sprinkle over the chopped peanuts, if using, and serve with limes halves to squeeze over.

For summer rice salad, make the kachumber as above and place in a bowl with 400 g (13 oz) cool, cooked basmati rice. Toss to mix well and serve with Crispy Poppadums (see page 190) and the pickle of your choice. For a treat, stir in 200 g (7 oz) cooked peeled prawns as well.

rice & bread

aubergine & tomato rice

Serves **4**

Preparation time **15 minutes**,
  plus soaking and standing

Cooking time **20–25 minutes**

275 g (9 oz) **basmati rice**

4 tablespoons **vegetable oil**

2 tablespoons **ghee**

4 **shallots**, finely chopped

2 **garlic cloves**, finely chopped

1 **cinnamon stick**

4 **green cardamom pods**

3 **cloves**

2 teaspoons **cumin seeds**

1 **aubergine**, trimmed and cut
  into 1 cm (½ inch) dice

4 **ripe tomatoes**, skinned,
  deseeded and finely
  chopped

2 teaspoons **salt**

1 teaspoon **pepper**

600 ml (1 pint) boiling **water**

6 tablespoons finely chopped
  coriander leaves

Wash the rice in several changes of cold water, drain and leave to soak in a bowl of cold water for 20 minutes. Drain thoroughly and set aside.

Heat the oil and ghee in a heavy-based saucepan over a medium heat and fry the shallots, garlic, cinnamon stick, cardamom pods, cloves and cumin seeds for 4–5 minutes until soft and fragrant. Add the diced aubergine and stir-fry over a medium heat for 4–5 minutes.

Add the tomatoes and drained rice and stir to mix well. Add the salt and pepper, and pour over the measurement boiling water. Bring to the boil. Cover the pan tightly, reduce the heat to low and cook for 10–12 minutes. Remove from the heat and leave to stand, covered, for 10 minutes.

Uncover and fluff up the grains of rice with a fork. Stir in the coriander and serve immediately with whisked natural yogurt and Crisp Poppadums (see below).

For crisp poppadums, to serve as an accompaniment, heat about 250 ml (8 fl oz) vegetable oil in a deep frying pan or wok until it is hot. Working in batches, slide 1 shop-bought dried poppadum into the pan and with the assistance of 2 spatulas, gently press the edges down to retain the shape. The poppadum should cook in 5–6 seconds. Remove using both spatulas and drain on kitchen paper. Repeat until you have enough poppadums. To serve, sprinkle them lightly with a little paprika and scatter over a small handful of chopped coriander.

biryani

Serves **4**
Preparation time **25 minutes**
Cooking time **about 40 minutes**

3 **onions**
2 **garlic cloves**, chopped
25 g (1 oz) **fresh root ginger**,
  peeled and roughly chopped
2 teaspoons **ground turmeric**
¼ teaspoon **ground cloves**
½ teaspoon **dried chilli flakes**
¼ teaspoon **ground
  cinnamon**
2 teaspoons **medium curry
  paste**
1 tablespoon **lemon juice**
2 teaspoons **caster sugar**
300 g (10 oz) **lean chicken,
  turkey breast** or **lamb fillet,**
  cut into small pieces
6 tablespoons **vegetable oil**
1 small **cauliflower**, cut into
  small florets
2 **bay leaves**
300 g (10 oz) **basmati rice**
750 ml (1¼ pints) **chicken** or
  vegetable stock
1 tablespoon **nigella seeds**
salt and **pepper**
2 tablespoons toasted **flaked
  almonds**, to garnish

Chop 1 onion roughly and put in a food processor with the garlic, ginger, turmeric, cloves, chilli flakes, cinnamon, curry paste, lemon juice, sugar and salt and pepper. Blend to a thick paste and turn into a bowl. Add the meat to the bowl, mix well and set aside.

Slice the second onion thinly. Heat 5 tablespoons of the oil in a large frying pan and fry the onion slices until deep golden and crisp. Drain on kitchen paper.

Chop the third onion. Add the cauliflower to the frying pan and fry gently for 5 minutes. Add the chopped onion and fry gently, stirring, for about 5 minutes until the cauliflower is softened and golden. Drain on kitchen paper. Heat the remaining oil in the pan. Tip in the meat and marinade and fry gently for 5 minutes, stirring.

Stir in the bay leaves, rice and stock and bring to the boil. Reduce the heat and simmer very gently, stirring occasionally, for 10–12 minutes until the rice is tender and the stock absorbed, adding a little water to the pan if the mixture is dry before the rice is cooked. Stir in the nigella seeds. Return the cauliflower to the pan and heat through.

Pile on to serving plates and serve scattered with the crisp onion and toasted almonds. Serve with a Cucumber & Mint Raita (see below).

For cucumber & mint raita, to serve as an accompaniment, gently mix the following in a bowl: 175 ml (6fl oz) natural yogurt, 75 g (3 oz) cucumber, deseeded and coarsely grated, 2 tablespoons chopped mint, a pinch of ground cumin and lemon juice and salt to taste. Leave to stand for 30 minutes.

spicy rice with yogurt & cucumber

Serves **4**

Preparation time **25 minutes, plus standing**

Cooking time **about 15 minutes**

300 g (10 oz) **basmati rice**
4 tablespoons **ghee**
2 teaspoons **salt**
600 ml (1 pint) boiling **water**
2 **green chillies**, deseeded
1 tablespoon finely chopped **fresh root ginger**
400 ml (14 fl oz) **natural set yogurt**, whisked
6 tablespoons finely chopped **coriander leaves**
1 teaspoon **sugar**
½ **cucumber**, finely diced
1 teaspoon **urad dhal** (optional)
2 teaspoons **mustard seeds**
2 teaspoons **cumin seeds**
2 **dried red chillies**
6–8 **fresh curry leaves**
2 **garlic cloves**, very thinly sliced

Place the rice in a heavy-based saucepan with 1 tablespoon of the ghee and 1 teaspoon of the salt and pour over the measurement water. Bring to the boil, turn the heat down to very low, cover tightly and cook for 10–12 minutes. Remove from the heat and rest for 12–15 minutes, covered.

Blend the green chillies and ginger in a mini food processor or blender with 4 tablespoons water until smooth.

Place the yogurt in a wide mixing bowl and add the chilli mixture along with the chopped coriander, sugar, remaining salt and cucumber. Mix well.

Fluff up the grains with a fork. Spoon in the yogurt mixture and toss to mix well.

Heat the remaining ghee in a medium frying pan and when hot add the urad dhal, if using, and the mustard and cumin seeds. As soon as they start to pop, add the dried red chillies, curry leaves and garlic. Stir-fry for 30–40 seconds, remove from the heat and pour over the rice. Toss to mix well and serve warm, with Kachumber (see page 186) and the pickle of your choice, if liked.

For pickled green chillies, to serve as an accompaniment, pack 300 g (10 oz) sliced green chillies in a sterilized glass jar with a tight-fitting vinegar-proof lid. Mix 125 ml (4 fl oz) white wine vinegar, 250 ml (8 fl oz) water, 1 tablespoon sea salt and 5 tablespoons caster sugar until the sugar has dissolved. Pour the vinegar pickling liquid over the chillies to cover. Seal and store in the refrigerator for 4–5 days before using.

cumin & pea rice

Serves **4**

Preparation time **5 minutes**, **plus standing**

Cooking time **12–15 minutes**

275 g (9 oz) **basmati rice**
3 tablespoons **ghee**
10–12 **fresh curry leaves**
2 teaspoons **cumin seeds**
1 **dried red chilli**
1 **cinnamon stick**
50 g (2 oz) **toasted cashew nuts**
200 g (7 oz) **fresh** or **frozen peas**
600 ml (1 pint) boiling **vegetable** or **chicken stock**
salt

Place the rice in a wide sieve and rinse under cold running water. Drain thoroughly and set aside.

Heat the ghee in a heavy saucepan over a medium heat and add the curry leaves, cumin seeds, chilli, cinnamon stick and cashew nuts. Stir-fry for 1–2 minutes, then add the rice, peas and stock.

Season well with salt, bring to the boil, stir and cover the pan tightly. Reduce the heat to low and cook for 10–12 minutes. Remove from the heat and leave to stand, covered, for 10–12 minutes.

Fluff up the grains of rice with a fork. Serve immediately.

For coconut rice with curry leaves, heat 2 tablespoons vegetable oil in a heavy-based saucepan and add 1 teaspoon black mustard seeds, 2 teaspoons cumin seeds, 1 dried chilli, 12–14 fresh curry leaves and 275 g (9 oz) basmati rice. Stir-fry for 30 seconds, then add 400 ml (14 fl oz) hot water and 200 ml (7 fl oz) coconut milk. Stir to mix well and bring to the boil. Reduce the heat to low, cover tightly and cook for 10–12 minutes. Remove from the heat and leave to stand, undisturbed, for 10–12 minutes. Fluff up the grains of rice with a fork and serve.

pilau with split mung beans

Serves **4**

Preparation time **15 minutes**,
  plus standing

Cooking time **15–20 minutes**

2 tablespoons **ghee** or
  vegetable oil

200 g (7 oz) **dried yellow
  split mung beans**, rinsed
  and drained

200 g (7 oz) **basmati rice**,
  rinsed and drained

6–8 **black peppercorns**

2 teaspoons **cumin seeds**

4 **garlic cloves**, finely
  chopped

2 teaspoons **salt**

¼ teaspoon **ground turmeric**

1 litre (1¾ pints) boiling **water**

Heat the ghee or oil in a heavy-based saucepan over
a medium heat. Add the split beans and rice and stir-fry
gently for 1–2 minutes. Add the peppercorns, cumin seeds,
garlic, salt and turmeric and stir-fry for 1–2 minutes.

Pour in the measurement boiling water. Bring to the boil,
cover tightly and reduce the heat to low. Allow to cook,
covered and undisturbed, for 12–15 minutes. Remove from
the heat (without removing the lid) and leave to stand for
12–15 minutes.

Fluff up the grains with a fork. Serve with natural yogurt
and Pickled Green Chillies (see page 194), Lime Pickle
(see page 172) or Mango Chutney (see below).

For homemade mango chutney, to serve as an
accompaniment, heat 2 tablespoons vegetable oil in
a large, deep pan, add 2 sliced onions and fry for a few
minutes until soft. Stir in 2 teaspoons grated fresh root
ginger and cook, stirring frequently, for 8–10 minutes until
the onion is golden. Add 1 cinnamon stick, 1 teaspoon
each ground cumin and ground coriander and 2 teaspoons
nigella seeds and stir-fry for 2–3 minutes until toasted.
Stir in 1 teaspoon ground turmeric and 1 sliced red chilli,
and add the juice of 1 lemon and 1 kg (2 lb) diced mango
flesh. Pour in 400 ml (14 fl oz) water and 300 ml (10 fl oz)
white wine vinegar, add 400 g (13 oz) caster sugar and
2 teaspoons salt, cover and cook for 30 minutes. Take off
the lid, stir and simmer, uncovered, for about 30 minutes
(it may take longer), stirring frequently until the chutney
is thick and set. Spoon into sterilized jars and, once cool,
store in the refrigerator for up to 1 month.

saffron & cardamom pilau

Serves **4**

Preparation time **5 minutes**,
  plus standing

Cooking time **12–15 minutes**

275 g (9 oz) **basmati rice**
3 tablespoons **ghee**
1 **cinnamon stick**
6–8 **green cardamom pods**
10 **black peppercorns**
1 **dried bay leaf**
3 **cloves**
1 teaspoon **ground turmeric**
large pinch of **saffron threads**
  (about 1 teaspoon)
600 ml (1 pint) boiling
  vegetable or **chicken stock**
salt

Place the rice in a wide sieve, rinse under cold running water, drain thoroughly and set aside.

Heat the ghee in a heavy saucepan over a medium heat and add the cinnamon, cardamom, peppercorns, bay leaf and cloves. Stir-fry for 1–2 minutes, then add the rice, turmeric, saffron and stock.

Season well with salt, bring to the boil, stir and cover the pan tightly. Reduce the heat to low and cook for 10–12 minutes. Remove from the heat and leave to stand, covered, for 10–12 minutes.

Fluff up the grains of rice with a fork. Serve immediately.

For aromatic prawn pilau, heat 2 tablespoons ghee in a heavy-based saucepan over a high heat. Add 2 sliced onions and stir-fry for 12–15 minutes over a medium heat. Add 1 cinnamon stick, 2 teaspoons cumin seeds, 4 cloves, 4 lightly crushed green cardamom pods and 8–10 black peppercorns. Stir-fry for 2–3 minutes, then add 275 g (9 oz) washed, drained basmati rice and 400 g (13 oz) raw, peeled tiger prawns and stir for a minute or so until the grains are well coated. Pour over 600 ml (1 pint) vegetable stock. Season well with salt and pepper and bring to the boil. Cover the pan tightly, reduce the heat to low and cook for 10–12 minutes. Remove from the heat and leave to stand, covered, for 10–12 minutes. Uncover and fluff up the grains of rice with a fork. Serve immediately.

spiced vegetable rice

Serves **4**

Preparation time **10–12 minutes, plus standing**

Cooking time **12–15 minutes**

275 g (9 oz) **basmati rice**

2 tablespoons **vegetable oil**

2 tablespoons **ghee**

50 g (2 oz) **shop-bought crispy fried onions**

1 **cinnamon stick**

4 **green cardamom pods**

3 **cloves**

2 teaspoons **cumin seeds**

1 teaspoon **garlic paste**

200 g (7 oz) **baby spinach leaves**, roughly chopped

1 **tomato**, deseeded and roughly chopped

6 tablespoons finely chopped **dill**

600 ml (1 pint) boiling **water**

salt and **pepper**

Place the rice in a wide sieve, rinse under cold running water, drain thoroughly and set aside.

Heat the oil and ghee in a heavy saucepan over a medium heat and add the crispy onions, spices, garlic paste, spinach and tomato. Stir-fry for 1–2 minutes, then add the rice and dill.

Season well with salt and pepper and pour over the measurement boiling water. Bring to the boil, stir and cover the pan tightly. (If the lid is not very tight, cover the pan with aluminium foil before putting the lid on.) Reduce the heat to low and cook for 10–12 minutes. Remove the pan from the heat and leave to stand, covered, for 10–12 minutes.

Fluff up the grains of rice with a fork. Serve immediately with the raita of your choice, poppadums and pickles.

For sweetcorn raita, to serve as an accompaniment, heat 3 tablespoons vegetable oil in a large nonstick frying pan over a medium heat. Add 1 teaspoon each of black mustard seeds, chopped garlic, grated fresh root ginger and 1 finely chopped red chilli and stir-fry for 2–3 minutes until fragrant. Stir in ½ red pepper, cored, deseeded and finely chopped, 400 g (13 oz) fresh sweetcorn kernels and 2–3 tablespoons water and stir-fry for 3–4 minutes. Season with salt, remove from the heat and leave to cool. Whisk 250 ml (8 fl oz) natural yogurt until smooth and transfer to a large bowl. Add the red pepper and sweetcorn mixture and a small handful of finely chopped coriander and stir to mix well. Cover and chill until ready to serve.

paratha

Makes **12**
Preparation time **20 minutes**,
 plus resting
Cooking time **24 minutes**

225 g (7½ oz) **wholemeal
 flour,** plus extra for dusting
100 g (3½ oz) **plain flour**
1 teaspoon **ground
 cardamom**
2 teaspoons **salt**
250 g (8 oz) warm **buttermilk**
125 ml (4 fl oz) **sunflower oil**

Sift the flours into a large mixing bowl and add the cardamom and salt. Work in the buttermilk and 1 tablespoon of the oil to make a soft dough. Knead on a lightly floured surface for 10 minutes and form into a ball. Cover with a damp cloth and leave to rest for 20 minutes.

Divide the dough into 12 balls and roll each one out into a 15 cm (6 inch) disc. Brush a paratha with a little oil, fold in half and then brush again. Fold in half again to form a triangle, dust with a little flour and flatten with a rolling pin to make a 15 cm (6 inch) triangle. Repeat with the remaining breads.

Heat a nonstick ridged griddle pan or frying pan over a medium heat. Brush with a little oil and cook each paratha for 1 minute, pressing down with a spatula. Turn it over, brush with a little more oil and cook for a further 1 minute.

Remove each paratha and keep warm wrapped in foil while you cook the remaining breads. Serve warm with a raita of your choice.

For garlic parathas, add 2 garlic cloves, crushed, in the first step when you make the dough.

puri

Makes **12**
Preparation time **20 minutes**
Cooking time **5–10 minutes**

200 g (7 oz) **chapatti flour**
1 teaspoon **salt**
2½ tablespoons **vegetable oil**
150 ml (¼ pint) warm **water**
vegetable or **sunflower oil**,
  for deep-frying
Coriander Chutney, to serve
  (see page 184)

Place the flour and salt in a wide mixing bowl, making a well in the centre. Pour in 2 tablespoons of the oil and work it into the flour mixture with your fingertips. Gradually add the measurement warm water to the flour (a few tablespoons at a time) and bring the mixture together to form a firm dough that is slightly wet and sticky. Knead the dough in the bowl for 3–4 minutes until smooth and no longer sticky. Drizzle over the remaining oil and knead again for 1 minute until smooth.

Divide the dough into 12 portions and roll each one into a small ball. On a lightly floured surface, flatten each ball and roll into an even, thin, 12 cm (5 inch) disc with a rolling pin, sprinkling on a little extra flour if sticking.

Fill a wide, deep saucepan or wok with the oil (about 5 cm/2 inches deep) and heat over a medium-high heat to 190°C (375°F), using a cooking thermometer. Using a flat, metal slotted spoon, lower a puri into the oil, pushing it gently with the back of the spoon to submerge it completely in the oil. The bread will begin to puff up. Cook for about 10 seconds, then carefully flip it over for another 8–10 seconds.

Remove with the slotted spoon and drain on kichen paper while you cook the remaining puris, making sure that the temperature remains at 190°C (375°F). Serve immediately with Coriander Chutney, a raita or pickle of your choice.

roti

Makes **8**
Preparation time **10 minutes**
Cooking time **16–24 minutes**

250 g (8 oz) **chapatti flour**
1 teaspoon **salt**
3 tablespoons **vegetable oil**
150 ml (¼ pint) warm **water**

Put the flour in a mixing bowl with the salt. Drizzle over the oil and the measurement warm water and knead in the bowl with your hands until the dough is smooth and elastic. Turn out on to a lightly floured surface and knead for another 1–2 minutes.

Divide the dough into 8 portions and roll each one into a smooth ball. Roll out each ball into a thin disc on a lightly floured surface until about 20 cm (8 inches) in diameter. If it begins to stick, sprinkle over some more flour.

Place a large, flat, nonstick frying pan over a medium-high heat and when hot cook the roti for 2–3 minutes, turning halfway through and pressing it down with a flat spatula to cook evenly. It will get lightly browned in places and should look dry.

Transfer to a plate and cover with foil and a clean tea towel to keep warm while you make the remaining rotis. Serve immediately.

For spinach rotis, blanch 100 g (3½ oz) chopped spinach leaves in boiling water for 1–2 minutes or until wilted, drain thoroughly and squeeze out any extra liquid. Add to the flour and salt in the above recipe, with 2 teaspoons dried chilli flakes and 2 teaspoons cumin seeds, before drizzling over the oil and warm water. Proceed as above.

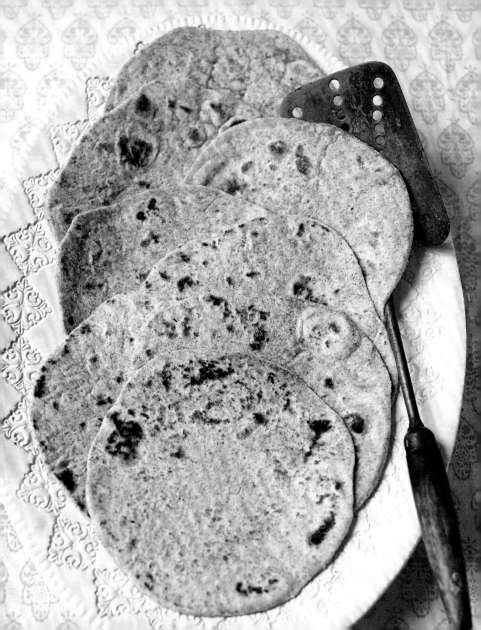

gram flour roti

Makes **8**
Preparation time **20 minutes,
plus resting**
Cooking time **8–16 minutes**

115 g (3¾ oz) **wholemeal
flour**
115 g (3¾ oz) **gram flour**
2 teaspoons **salt**
2 tablespoons finely chopped
coriander leaves
2 **red chillies**, finely chopped
2 teaspoons **cumin seeds**
1 teaspoon crushed **coriander
seeds**
1 teaspoon **ground turmeric**
90 ml (3¼ fl oz) melted **ghee**
or **butter**, plus extra for
brushing
200 ml (7 fl oz) **water**

Sift the flours and salt into a mixing bowl. Add the
coriander, chillies, cumin seeds, crushed coriander
seeds, turmeric and melted ghee or butter. Mix and
gradually add the measurement water to form a soft,
pliable dough. Knead on a lightly floured work surface
for 1–2 minutes, then allow to rest for 10 minutes.

Divide the mixture into 8 balls and roll out each one
into a 12–15 cm (5–6 inch) disc. Brush the tops with
melted ghee or butter.

Heat a nonstick frying pan over a high heat. When hot,
cook the rotis, one at a time, for 1–2 minutes on each
side, pressing down with a spatula for even cooking.
Remove the roti from the pan, and keep warm, wrapped
in foil, while you cook the remainder. Serve warm with
chutney, if liked.

For South Indian coconut chutney, to serve as an
accompaniment, soak 1 tablespoon yellow split lentils
in cold water for 2–3 hours, drain and set aside. Put
200 g (7 oz) freshly grated coconut, 2 sliced green
chillies and 1 teaspoon sea salt in a food processor
and blend to a fine paste, adding a little cold water
if needed. Transfer to a bowl. Heat 2 tablespoons
vegetable oil in a small frying pan over a low heat and
add 2 teaspoons black mustard seeds and the reserved
lentils. Cover the pan and fry gently for 3–4 minutes
until you hear the mustard seeds start to pop. Add
6–8 fresh curry leaves and 1 dried red chilli, roughly
broken, and stir-fry for 1 minute. Pour the lentil mixture
into the coconut mixture, add 1 teaspoon tamarind
paste and stir to mix well. Serve immediately, or store,
covered, in the refrigerator for up to 4 days.

potato & cauliflower paratha

Makes **8**

Preparation time **30 minutes**, **plus resting**

Cooking time **35–50 minutes**

225 g (7½ oz) **wholemeal flour**

100 g (3½ oz) **plain flour**

1 teaspoon **ground cardamom**

2 teaspoons **salt**

250 ml (8 fl oz) warm **buttermilk**

150 g (5 oz) **ghee**, melted

Filling

2 tablespoons **vegetable oil**

2 teaspoons **cumin seeds**

1 tablespoon **hot curry powder**

4 **garlic cloves**, crushed

2 teaspoons finely grated **fresh root ginger**

150 g (5 oz) **cauliflower**, very finely chopped

2 teaspoons **salt**

2 **potatoes**, boiled and roughly mashed

6 tablespoons finely chopped **coriander leaves**

Make the potato filling mixture. Heat the oil in a large frying pan over a medium heat. Add the cumin seeds, curry powder, garlic, ginger and cauliflower and stir-fry for 8–10 minutes. Add the salt and the mashed potatoes and stir well to mix evenly. Remove from the heat and stir in the coriander. Leave to cool.

Sift the flours into a large bowl and add the cardamom and salt. Make a well in the centre and pour in the buttermilk and 2 tablespoons of the ghee. Work into the flour mixture to make a soft dough. Knead on a lightly floured surface for 10 minutes, and form into a ball. Put in a bowl, cover with a damp cloth and leave to rest for 20 minutes.

Divide the dough into 8 balls and roll each one into a 15 cm (6 inch) round. Place one-eighth of the potato mixture in the centre of each, then fold the edges into the centre to enclose the filling. Press down gently and with a lightly floured rolling pin roll out to make a 15 cm (6 inch) paratha. Repeat until you have 8 parathas.

Heat a nonstick, cast-iron, flat griddle or heavy-based frying pan over a medium heat. Brush each paratha and the griddle or frying pan with a little melted ghee. Put a paratha in the pan and cook for 2–3 minutes, pressing down with a spatula. Turn over, brush with a little more ghee and cook for another 1–2 minutes or until flecked with light brown spots. Remove and keep warm in foil while you cook the remaining breads.

For pea & potato parathas, replace the cauliflower with 150 g (5 oz) defrosted, frozen peas and proceed as above.

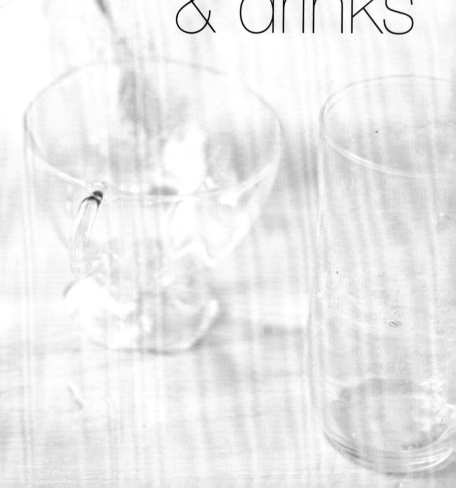

sweets
& drinks

mango & cardamom kulfi

Serves **4**

Preparation time **10 minutes**,
   plus freezing

200 ml (7 fl oz) **sweetened
   condensed milk**
250 ml (8 fl oz) **double cream**
150 g (5 oz) **canned
   Alphonso** or **Kesar mango
   purée**
1 teaspoon finely crushed
   cardamom seeds
2 tablespoons roughly
   chopped **pistachio nuts**
2 tablespoons **pomegranate
   seeds**

Place the condensed milk, cream, mango purée and
cardamom into a wide mixing bowl and, using an
electric (or hand) whisk, beat until thickened.

Spoon the mixture into 4 individual dariole moulds,
cover with foil and clingfilm, and freeze for 6–8 hours
or overnight.

Dip the moulds in hot water for a few seconds and,
using a palette knife, remove the desserts on to
serving plates.

Sprinkle over the pistachios and pomegranate seeds
and serve immediately.

For saffron & pistachio kulfi ice-pops, mix
1 teaspoon saffron threads with 4 tablespoons hot milk
in a jug. Place 400 ml (14 fl oz) sweetened condensed
milk in a bowl with 250 ml (8 fl oz) double cream and,
using an electric (or hand) whisk, beat until thickened.
Stir in the saffron mixture. Spoon the mixture into
6 ice-pop moulds and freeze for 6–8 hours or overnight.
When ready to serve, dip the moulds in hot water for
a few seconds, remove the ice-pops and serve.

almond, pistachio & rice pudding

Serves **4**

Preparation time **10 minutes, plus resting**

Cooking time **about 25 minutes**

2 litres (3½ pints) **milk**

150 g (3¼ oz) **basmati rice**

100 g (3½ oz) **golden caster sugar**

1 teaspoon **ground cardamom**

6 tablespoons finely chopped **blanched almonds**

6 tablespoons finely chopped **pistachio nuts**

Bring the milk to the boil in a heavy-based wide saucepan. Add the rice and cook over a medium heat, stirring often, for 18–20 minutes or until tender.

Add the sugar and stir and cook for 3–4 minutes.

Remove from the heat and stir in the ground cardamom and three-quarters of the nuts. Cover and leave to rest for 20 minutes before serving, scattered with the remaining nuts.

For chilled rosewater & pistachio rice pudding, boil 2 litres (3½ pints) milk in a heavy-based saucepan, add 85 g (3¼ oz) basmati rice and cook over a medium heat, stirring often, for 18–20 minutes or until the rice is tender. Add 100 g (3½ oz) caster sugar, stir and cook for 3–4 minutes or until dissolved. Remove from the heat and stir in 2 tablespoons rosewater, 100 g (3½ oz) finely chopped pistachio nuts and a grating of nutmeg. Leave to cool, cover and chill for 4–6 hours before serving, decorated with edible rose petals.

nut & fruit dessert pots

Serves **4**

Preparation time **10 minutes,
plus standing and chilling**

200 g (7 oz) **ready-to-eat
dried apricots**, roughly
chopped

100 g (3½ oz) **golden
sultanas**

100 ml (3½ fl oz) **orange juice**

300 ml (½ pint) **double cream**

4 tablespoons **golden caster
sugar**

1 teaspoon **rosewater**

4 tablespoons finely chopped
pistachio nuts

4 tablespoons finely chopped
walnuts

4 tablespoons finely chopped
hazelnuts

Place the apricots in a bowl with the sultanas and
orange juice. Cover and leave to stand for 20 minutes.

Whisk the cream, sugar and rosewater in a separate
bowl until softly peaked. Fold in three-quarters of the
chopped nuts.

Divide the apricot mixture between the bases of
4 dessert glasses or pots. Spoon over the cream
mixture and chill in the refrigerator for 3–4 hours.

Decorate each dessert with the remaining nuts and
serve immediately.

For spiced fruit & nut granola, in a saucepan bring
60 g (2¼ oz) butter and 4 tablespoons maple syrup
to a simmer, then remove from the heat. In a bowl, mix
200 g (7 oz) rolled oats, 100 g (3½ oz) each coarsely
chopped pistachio nuts and desiccated coconut and a
pinch of salt. Stir in the liquid and mix until everything
is coated. Spread the mix evenly on a lined baking sheet.
Bake in a preheated oven, 180°C (350°F), Gas Mark 4,
for 20–25 minutes. Remove and stir it every 5 minutes
so that everything gets evenly roasted and to avoid any
burning. When golden and crispy, remove it from the
oven. Put it back in the bowl and mix in 1 tablespoon
ground cinnamon, 1 teaspoon vanilla extract, ½ teaspoon
ground cardamom, 8 each coarsely chopped dried figs
and Medjool dates and 100 g (3½ oz) dried cranberries.
When cooled, store the granola in an airtight container
and serve with yogurt.

goan coconut layer cake

Serves **4**

Preparation time **10 minutes**, **plus chilling**

Cooking time **1¾ hours– 2¼ hours**

400 ml (14 fl oz) **coconut milk**

300 g (10 oz) **golden caster sugar**

10 **egg yolks**, lightly beaten

200 g (7 oz) **plain flour**

½ teaspoon grated **nutmeg**

1 teaspoon **ground cardamom**

pinch of **ground cloves**

¼ teaspoon **ground cinnamon**

100 g (3½ oz) **butter**, plus extra for greasing

vanilla ice cream, to serve

Lightly grease and line the base and sides of a 16 cm (6¼ inch) nonstick cake tin with baking paper.

Pour the coconut milk into a saucepan and stir in the sugar. Heat gently for 8–10 minutes, stirring until the sugar has dissolved. Remove from the heat and gradually drizzle in the beaten eggs, whisking all the time so that the eggs do not scramble and the mixture is smooth. Sift in the flour, add the spices and stir to make a smooth batter.

Melt the butter in a small saucepan, then spoon a tablespoon into the prepared tin and spread over the base. Pour one-eighth of the batter into the tin and spread to coat evenly. Place in a preheated oven, 200°C (400°F), Gas Mark 6, and bake for 10–12 minutes until set.

Remove from the oven and brush another spoonful of the melted butter over the top, followed by another one-eighth of the batter. Return to the oven and cook for 10–12 minutes or until set.

Repeat this process until all the butter and batter is used up, baking for a further 20–25 minutes or until the top is golden brown and the cake is firmly set. Leave to cool in the tin, then remove, cover with clingfilm and chill in the refrigerator for 4–6 hours. Serve cut into thin wedges, with vanilla ice cream, if liked.

For Goan coconut pancakes, mix 12 tablespoons freshly grated coconut with 2 tablespoons golden raisins, 4 tablespoons palm sugar and ¼ teaspoon ground cardamom in a bowl. Divide between 6 shop-bought pancakes and roll up to enclose the filling. Lightly dust with icing sugar before serving.

bengali caramel yogurt

Serves **4**

Preparation time **5 minutes**, **plus setting and chilling**

Cooking time **about 12 minutes**

400 g (13 fl oz) can **evaporated milk**

200 ml (7 fl oz) **condensed milk**

2 tablespoons **caster sugar**

100 ml (3½ fl oz) **natural yogurt**, whisked

Heat the evaporated milk and condensed milk in a saucepan and bring to the boil. Turn the heat to low, stir and simmer gently for 10 minutes until well mixed, then remove from the heat.

Meanwhile, in a small saucepan, heat the sugar over a low heat until it turns golden and starts to caramelize. Remove from the heat, add the caramelized sugar mixture to the milk mixture and stir to mix well. When the milk mixture is just warm, stir in the yogurt and mix well.

Pour into 4 dessert bowls, cover with clingfilm and place in a warm place (such as a turned-off oven) for 8–10 hours, or overnight, until lightly set.

Transfer to a refrigerator and chill for 4–6 hours before serving.

For frozen mango yogurt, stir a 400 g (13 oz) can sweetened condensed milk into a bowl with 200 g (7 oz) canned mango purée and 400 ml (14 fl oz) Greek yogurt. Spoon the mixture into a loaf tin or freezer-proof container, wrap well in clingfilm and freeze overnight or until solid. Remove from the freezer 15–20 minutes before serving, to make it easier to scoop.

banana & cardamom lassi

Serves **4**
Preparation time **10 minutes**

500 ml (17 fl oz) **natural
  yogurt**
1–2 tablespoons **caster sugar**
  (or to taste)
2 **bananas,** roughly chopped
200 ml (7 fl oz) ice-cold **water**
½ teaspoon finely crushed
  cardamom seeds
4 scoops **vanilla ice cream,**
  to serve (optional)

Place all the ingredients (except the ice cream) in a
food processor or blender and blend for a few minutes
until frothy and smooth.

Pour into 4 chilled glasses and serve immediately with
a scoop of vanilla ice cream, if liked.

For mango & cardamom lassi, place 200 g (7 oz)
canned mango purée in a blender with 400 ml (14 fl oz)
natural yogurt, 1 teaspoon crushed cardamom seeds,
1 tablespoon caster sugar and 100 ml (3½ fl oz)
ice-cold water. Blend until smooth, pour into chilled
glasses and serve.

rose & vermicelli milkshake

Serves **4**

Preparation time **20 minutes, plus soaking**

2 teaspoons **basil seeds (tukmaria)**

200 ml (7 fl oz) cold **water**

10 g (1/3 oz) **very fine rice vermicelli**

125 ml (4 fl oz) **Indian rose syrup**

1 litre (1¾ pints) **milk**, chilled

4 scoops **vanilla ice cream**

Place the basil seeds in a bowl and pour over the measurement water. Leave to soak for 15 minutes or until swollen and jelly-like. Drain and set aside.

Meanwhile, break the vermicelli into small pieces and cook according to the packet instructions. Drain and refresh under cold running water.

Pour equal amounts of the syrup into the bases of 4 large glasses. Divide the hydrated basil seeds and the vermicelli between the glasses. Pour over the chilled milk and top each one with a scoop of ice cream.

Serve immediately with long-handled spoons.

For rose & banana milkshake, place 800 ml (1 pint 7 fl oz) chilled milk in a blender with 2 chopped bananas and 4 tablespoons Indian rose syrup. Blend until frothy and smooth. Pour into chilled glasses and top each with a scoop of vanilla ice cream.

lemon grass & ginger tea

Serves **4**

Preparation time **5 minutes**,
plus infusing

Cooking time **about 5
minutes**

4 **lemon grass stalks**, plus
extra to garnish (optional)

**small knob of fresh root
ginger,** thinly sliced

600 ml (1 pint) **water**

1 **green tea bag**

clear honey, to serve

Cut the lemon grass stalks into 4 cm (1¾ inch) lengths
and crush them with the flat side of a large knife.

Place the lemon grass in a saucepan with the ginger
and the measurement water. Bring to the boil, then add
the green tea bag. Remove from the heat and allow to
infuse for 3–4 minutes.

Pour through a fine sieve or strainer into heatproof
glasses or cups. Garnish with stalks of lemon grass,
if liked, and serve with honey to sweeten.

For chilled lemon grass & rum cocktail, finely chop
the bases of 4 lemon grass stalks and divide between
4 tall glasses. Divide 8 tablespoons of soft light brown
sugar and 8 sprigs of mint between them, then crush
with a muddler or the end of a rolling pin to release all
the flavours. Add 2 lime wedges to each glass, crush
the mixture a little more, then pour 50 ml (2 fl oz) dark
rum into each one. Fill the glasses with crushed ice and
top up with soda water.

iced lime & mint cooler

Serves **4**

Preparation time **10 minutes, plus chilling**

5 large **limes**
50 g (2 oz) **white caster sugar** (or to taste)
pinch of **salt** (optional)
250 ml (8 fl oz) cold **water**
350 ml (12 fl oz) **soda water**, chilled
¼ **cucumber,** sliced, plus 4 extra slices to serve
2 **sprigs of mint**, plus 4 extra sprigs to serve
crushed ice, to serve

Cut one of the limes into chunks. Place in a food processor or blender along with any juices from the chopping board and the juice of the remaining limes, the sugar, the salt, if using, and a little of the measurement water. Whizz to a purée, then add the rest of the water. Taste and add a little more sugar if necessary.

Pour into a jug, top up with the soda water, add the cucumber and mint, then chill until ready to serve.

Serve over crushed ice with a fresh slice of cucumber and a fresh sprig of mint for each glass.

For sparkling ginger & lime fizz, place the juice of 2 limes in a food processor or blender with 4 knobs of chopped, preserved stem ginger, 4 tablespoons syrup from the stem ginger jar and 800 ml (1 pint 7 fl oz) chilled soda or sparkling mineral water. Blend until well combined, pour immediately into 4 ice-filled tall glasses and serve immediately.

spiced milky tea

Serves **4**
Preparation time **5 minutes**,
  plus infusing
Cooking time **7–8 minutes**

600 ml (1 pint) **water**
200 ml (7 fl oz) **milk**
50 g (2 oz) **caster sugar**
2 **cinnamon sticks**
6 **cloves**
6 **green cardamom pods**,
  lightly crushed
1 teaspoon chopped **fresh**
  root ginger
1–2 tablespoons **Assam**
  loose-leaf tea

Pour the measurement water and milk into a saucepan with the sugar, cinnamon, cloves, cardamom and ginger. Bring to the boil then reduce the heat to low and simmer for 5–6 minutes.

Put the tea leaves in a teapot and pour in the spiced mixture. Allow to infuse for 4–5 minutes before serving, straining into teacups.

For hot cardamom coffee, place 6 crushed green cardamom pods in a saucepan with 600 ml (1 pint) milk, 1 tablespoon good-quality instant coffee and 1 tablespoon sugar (or to taste) and bring to the boil, whisking constantly. Once piping hot, strain into 4 mugs and serve immediately, adding more sugar if required.

index

acknowledgements

Senior Commissioning Editor Eleanor Maxfield
Managing Editor Sybella Stephens
Art Direction and Design Penny Stock
Photographer William Shaw
Home economist Denise Smart
Prop Stylist Liz Hippisley
Production Controller Allison Gonsalves

Photography copyright © Octopus Publishing Group
Stephen Conroy 10, 25, 29, 39, 69, 73, 75, 95, 129,
131, 159, 205; Will Heap 55, 59, 71, 109, 111, 117,
149, 153; Lis Parsons 91; William Reavell 65;
William Shaw 8, 13, 31, 139; Ian Wallace 83, 145, 161.
Shutterstock Arnon Polin 9. Thinkstock vikif 12.